Intermediate Arabic Reader

# روميو وجولييت

## Romeo and Juliet

lingualism

© 2018 by Matthew Aldrich

The author's moral rights have been asserted. All rights reserved. No part of this document may be reproduced or transmitted in any form or by any means, electronic, mechanical, photocopying, recording, or otherwise, without prior written permission of the publisher.

ISBN: 978-1-949650-03-7


Adapted from William Shakespeare's play *Romeo and Juliet* by Lilia Khachroum

Conceptualized and edited by Matthew Aldrich

Edited by Israa Ramadan and Lilia Khachroum

Illustrated by Marina Lobanova

Audio by Heba Salah Ali


website: www.lingualism.com

email: contact@lingualism.com

# Table of Contents

INTRODUCTION ................................................................... II
ACKNOWLEDGMENTS ......................................................... IV
AUDIO .............................................................................. IV
ANKI FLASHCARDS .............................................................. IV
**اَلْفَصْلُ الْأَوَّلُ** ........................................................... **1**
   VOCABULARY ............................................................... 10
   TRANSLATION .............................................................. 18
**اَلْفَصْلُ الثَّانِي** ......................................................... **24**
   VOCABULARY ............................................................... 32
   TRANSLATION .............................................................. 37
**اَلْفَصْلُ الثَّالِثُ** ........................................................ **42**
   VOCABULARY ............................................................... 51
   TRANSLATION .............................................................. 57
**اَلْفَصْلُ الرَّابِعُ** ........................................................ **63**
   VOCABULARY ............................................................... 70
   TRANSLATION .............................................................. 74
**اَلْفَصْلُ الْخَامِسُ** ..................................................... **79**
   VOCABULARY ............................................................... 88
   TRANSLATION .............................................................. 93
**اَلْفَصْلُ السَّادِسُ** .................................................... **100**
   VOCABULARY ............................................................. 110
   TRANSLATION ............................................................ 115
**اَلْفَصْلُ السَّابِعُ** ..................................................... **122**
   VOCABULARY ............................................................. 129
   TRANSLATION ............................................................ 133
**اَلْفَصْلُ الثَّامِنُ** ..................................................... **138**
   VOCABULARY ............................................................. 148
   TRANSLATION ............................................................ 153

# Introduction

The timeless love story of Romeo and Juliet has been brought to life for the first time as a novelized adaptation for learners of Arabic. This story was chosen as it is well known to Western audiences; being familiar with the characters and plot of a story will help you focus less on what the story is about and more on the language.

The story has been divided into eight chapters of similar, manageable length for learners. Accompanying audio, professionally recorded by a native speaker, is available to download free of charge from Lingualism.com.

Each chapter has three parts:

- The Arabic text, which is voweled (that is, written with tashkeel diacritics) to aid in recognition and pronunciation of each word.
- An extensive glossary which contains words and phrases the first time they appear in the book. All but very basic words are glossed.
- The English translation.

When the name of a character or place makes its first appearance in the book, it is shown in bold.

Words and phrases that appear in the vocabulary section (glossary) are underlined in the text with a subtle dotted line. They are organized by order of appearance and grouped by the page number on which they appear.

A noun or adjective will be listed in its singular form, and if its plural is irregular, this will be shown in parentheses.

A verb will be shown in its base form followed by a reference code in small square brackets. This corresponds to a table showing the verb's complete conjugation patterns in Lingualism's book Modern Standard Arabic Verbs. The masdar (gerund) of unaugmented (measure I) verbs is given in parentheses. The masdar for augmented verbs is also normally given when they appear in the book.

Many nouns (including masdars) and adjectives (including active and passive participles) act as adverbs in the indefinite accusative case or in conjunction with a preposition. These are often glossed as the basic form of the word, so you can see each word's original meaning and how it can be used as an adverb in context.

Abbreviations found in the glossary:

| | | | |
|---|---|---|---|
| *f.* | feminine | **pass.** | passive |
| ***coll.*** | collective | ***pl.*** | plural |

There are many ways to use the glossary, English translation, audio, and Anki flashcards (available separately at Lingualism.com) as pre-reading and post-reading tools to improve your overall comprehension of the Arabic text. It all depends on your learning style and what you find works best for you. For example, you can try listening to the audio before you read the text to see how much you understand going in. You can also read a chapter in English first, which will help you guess new vocabulary when you see it. You can study the vocabulary for each page or chapter before reading it. Alternatively, you can look up new words as you encounter them in the text, and then read the chapter again to see how many of the new words you can recall. You can refer to the English translation when you can't work out the overall meaning of a sentence, even if you know each word. In any case, multiple readings are recommended to build reading fluency and memorization of new vocabulary. Which strategy works best for you? Please let us know in the comments at **www.lingualism.com/raj**.

# Acknowledgments

I would like to thank all of those involved in the project. Lilia Khachroum did an amazing job adapting Shakespeare's play into a short novel in Arabic, all the while balancing the level of the grammar and vocabulary in order to keep it at an appropriate level for intermediate learners. She painstakingly wrote the original text with tashkeel and was of great help to me in translating the text into English. Israa Ramadan meticulously proofread the text and checked it against the audio. Marina Lobanova created beautiful illustrations to go along with each chapter. Heba Salah Ali brought the text to life by providing the accompanying audio. Thank you all!

Matthew Aldrich

# Audio

Access the **free**, accompanying **MP3s**, which can be downloaded or streamed from **www.lingualism.com/raj**.

# Anki Flashcards

Study the words and phrases from the glossary using Anki flashcards with audio.

*(Available as a separate purchase at Lingualism.com.)*

# اَلْفَصْلُ الْأَوَّلُ

يُحْكَى أَنَّ خِلافًا جادًّا نَشِبَ بَيْنَ عائِلَتَيْنِ مِنْ أَنْبَلِ عائِلاتِ مَدينَةِ **فيرونا** الْإيطاليَّةِ، عائِلَةِ **كابوليت** وَعائِلَةِ **مُنْتيغْيو** – عائِلَتانِ عَريقَتانِ. جَمَعَتْهُما عَداوَةٌ اِشْتَعَلَتْ نيرانُها مُنْذُ سَنَواتٍ طَويلَةٍ، حَتَّى أَنَّ أَسْبابَ الصِّراعِ بَيْنَهُما نُسِيَتْ مَعَ مُرورِ الزَّمَنِ، وَلَكِنَّ كَراهِيَّتُهُما ظَلَّتْ مُتَواصِلَةً كَأَنْ وُرِثَتْ مِنْ جيلٍ إِلَى جيلٍ.

بَدا **سَمْبْسونْ** وَكَأَنَّهُ يَتَجادَلُ مَعَ **غْريغْوري** وَسَطَ ساحَةٍ عامَّةٍ في فيرونا، وَلَكِنَّهُما في الْحَقيقَةِ، كانا يَتَحَدَّثانِ عَنْ أَعْدائِهِما اللَّدودينَ، عائِلَةِ مُنْتيغْيو!

سَمْبْسونْ وَغْريغوري هُما خادِمانِ لِعائِلَةِ كابوليتْ؛ جَمَعَهُما كُرْهٌ غَيْرُ مَسْبوقٍ لِعائِلَةِ مُنْتيغيو.

كانَ سَمْبْسون مُتَشَنِّجًا وَعَصَبِيًّا، أَمّا غْريغوري فَكانَ لا يُضَيِّعُ فُرْصَةً لِاسْتِفْزازِهِ وَجَوِّهِ لِلتَّباهي بِقُوَّتِهِ، وَمَهاراتِهِ الْقِتالِيَّةِ الَّتي سَيَفْتِكُ بِها بِأَفْرادِ عائِلَةِ مُنْتيغيو.

"لَنْ أَرْفِقَ بِرِجالِهِمْ... سَوْفَ أَقْتُلُهُمْ جَميعًا! أَمّا النِّساءُ... فَسَأَكونُ رَقيقًا وَمُهَذَّبًا مَعَهُنَّ... سَأَسْلُبُهُنَّ عُذْرِيَّتَهُنَّ!" صاحَ سَمْبْسون مُتَوَعِّدًا.

كُلَّما اسْتَفَزَّهُ غْريغوري، ازْدادَ حَماسَهُ أَكْثَرَ وَأَكْثَرَ، وَشَرَعَ في التَّوَعُّلِ وَالتَّهْديدِ. وَظَلّا هَكَذا إلى أَنْ لَمَحا مِنْ بَعيدٍ **أَبْراهامْ** بِرِفْقَةِ خادِمٍ ثانٍ لِعائِلَةِ مُنْتيغيو يَقْتَرِبانِ مِنْهُما شَيْئًا فَشَيْئًا.

ظَهَرَ الْقَلَقُ عَلى وَجْهِ غْريغوري، في حينٍ واصَلَ سَمْبْسون في لَهْجَتِهِ الْمُتَحَدِّيَةِ، إِلّا أَنَّهُ هَذِهِ الْمَرَّةَ لَمْ يُرِدْ مُخالَفَةَ الْقانونِ، فَنَظَرَ إلى غْريغوري قائِلًا: "يَجِبُ أَنْ يَكونَ الْقانونُ مَعَنا! عَلَيْهِما أَنْ يَبْدَآ هُما بِالشِّجارِ، وَهَكَذا سَيَحْمينا الْقانونُ..."

قَضَمَ سَمْبْسون إِصْبَعَهُ في حَرَكَةٍ مُسْتَفِزَّةٍ لا أَخْلاقِيَّةٍ. فَسَأَلَهُ أَبْراهام

وَقَدْ ظَهَرَ الْغَضَبُ فِي عَيْنَيْهِ عَمَّا إِذَا كَانَ يَقْصِدُ إِهَانَتَهُ هُوَ وَرَفِيقُهُ بِحَرَكَتِهِ تِلْكَ، فَأَجَابَهُ سَمْبْسُونٌ نَافِيًا: "لَا، لَمْ أَكُنْ أَقْصِدُكَ... وَلَكِنَّنِي فِعْلًا قُمْتُ بِحَرَكَةٍ لَا أَخْلَاقِيَّةٍ."

وَهُنَا تَدَخَّلَ غْرِيغُورِي مُتَّهِمًا أَبْرَاهَامَ بِمُحَاوَلَةِ بَدْءِ شِجَارٍ. وَنَجَحَ فِعْلًا فِي اسْتِفْزَازِ خَادِمَيْ عَائِلَةِ كَابُولِيت. سَلَّ الْجَمِيعُ سُيُوفَهُمْ وَبَدَؤُوا يَتَشَاجَرُونَ.

فِي هَذِهِ الْأَثْنَاءِ، وَصَلَ **بَنْفُولْيُو**، أَحَدُ أَقْرِبَاءِ عَائِلَةِ مُنْتِيغْيُو، فَسَلَّ بِدَوْرِهِ سَيْفَهُ صَارِخًا بِهِمْ: "أَوْقِفُوا هَذَا الشِّجَارَ فَوْرًا أَيُّهَا الْأَغْبِيَاءُ! هَيَّا أَلْقُوا بِسُيُوفِكُمْ حَالًا! أَنْتُمْ لَا تَعْرِفُونَ مَدَى خُطُورَةِ مَا تَفْعَلُونَهُ!"

بَنْفُولْيُو! دَعْكَ مِنْ هَؤُلَاءِ الْخَدَمِ وَتَعَالَ لِنَتَشَاجَرَ نِدًّا لِنِدٍّ... هَلْ لَدَيْكَ الْجُرْأَةُ الْكَافِيَةُ؟

اِلْتَفَتَ بَنْفُولْيُو لِيَكْتَشِفَ مَنْ يَتَحَدَّثُ مَعَهُ، فَوَجَدَ أَمَامَهُ **تِيبَالْتْ**، أَحَدَ أَقْرِبَاءِ عَائِلَةِ كَابُولِيت وَكَانَ مَشْهُورًا بِعَطْرَسَتِهِ وَعِنَادِهِ، فَحَاوَلَ أَنْ يُقْنِعَهُ بِالسِّلْمِ وَالْهُدُوءِ، إِلَّا أَنَّ تِيبَالْتْ أَجَابَهُ مُسْتَهْزِئًا:

"عَنْ أَيِّ سِلْمٍ تَتَحَدَّثُ؟ وَعَنْ أَيِّ هُدُوءٍ تَتَحَدَّثُ؟ أَتُشْهِرُ سِلَاحَكَ ثُمَّ

تَتَحَدَّثُ عَنِ السِّلْمِ؟ اَلسِّلْمُ؟... كَمْ أُكْرِهُ هَذِهِ الْكَلِمَةَ وَكَمْ أُكْرِهُ عَائِلَةَ مُنْتِيغْيُو، وَكَمْ أُكْرَهُكَ مَعَهُمْ! هَيَّا قَاتِلْنِي أَيُّهَا الْجَبَانُ! تَعَالَ!"

وَبَدَآ فِي الْقِتَالِ وَاجْتَشَدَتِ الْجَمَاهِيرُ تَهْتِفُ وَتُشَجِّعُ تَارَةً بَنْفُولْيُو وَتَارَةً تَيْبَالْتُ، تَارَةً هَاتِفَةً بِاسْمِ كَابُولِيت وَتَارَةً بِاسْمِ مُنْتِيغْيُو... إِلَى أَنْ هَرَعَ السَّيِّدَانِ كَابُولِيت وَمُنْتِيغْيُو بِرِفْقَةِ زَوْجَتَيْهِمَا إِلَى السَّاحَةِ لِاكْتِشَافِ سَبَبِ هَذَا الْاحْتِشَادِ وَالْهُتَافِ.

اِنْدَفَعَ الرَّجُلَانِ بِسُرْعَةِ الْبَرْقِ لِلِانْضِمَامِ إِلَى الْمَعْرَكَةِ، تَحْتَ مُحَاوَلَاتِ زَوْجَتَيْهِمَا لِتَهْدِئَةِ الْأَجْوَاءِ.

وَفَجْأَةً، ظَهَرَ أَمِيرُ الْبَلْدَةِ **أَسْكَالِيسْ** بِرِفْقَةِ رِجَالِهِ، وَقَدْ بَدَا الْغَضَبُ مُتَطَايِرًا مِنْ عَيْنَيْهِ، فَصَرَخَ مُخَاطِبًا رَعِيَّتَهُ: "أَيُّهَا الْمُتَمَرِّدُونَ! أَعْدَاءُ السَّلَامِ! يَا مَنْ يَتَجَرَّأُ وَيُشْهِرُ سِلَاحَهُ فِي وَجْهِ جَارِهِ! أَنْتُمْ لَسْتُمْ سِوَى وُحُوشًا ضَارِيَّةً تَسْتَمْتِعُ بِمُشَاهَدَةِ سَيَلَانِ دِمَاءِ بَعْضِكُمُ الْبَعْضِ! إِنَّكُمْ تُهَدِّدُونَ سَلَامَ الْمَدِينَةِ وَأَمْنِهَا! هَذِهِ الْمَرَّةُ الثَّالِثَةُ الَّتِي تَشْهَدُ فِيهَا مَدِينَتِي فَوْضَى عَارِمَةً بِسَبَبِ شِجَارِ عَائِلَتَيْ كَابُولِيت وَمُنْتِيغْيُو! كَفَاكُمْ شِجَارًا! سَتَمْتَثِلُونَ لِي حَالًا، وَسَتُلْقُونَ بِأَسْلِحَتِكُمْ، وَإِلَّا فَسَتَكُونُ عَاقِبَتُكُمُ التَّعْذِيبَ حَتَّى الْمَوْتِ."

أَلْقَى الْجَمِيعُ بِأَسْلِحَتِهِمْ أَرْضًا، وَقَدْ بَدَا الْخَوْفُ عَلَى وُجُوهِهِمْ، مُمْتَثِلِينَ لِأَوَامِرِ أَمِيرِهِمِ الْغَاضِبِ. هَدَأَ الْجَوُّ وَانْسَحَبَ الْكُلُّ مِنَ السَّاحَةِ، وَلَمْ يَبْقَ سِوَى السَّيِّدِ مُنْتِيغِيُو وَزَوْجَتِهِ وَبَنْفُولِيُو.

كَانَ السَّيِّدُ مُنْتِيغِيُو قَلِقًا بِشَأْنِ مَا حَدَثَ، فَسَرَدَ لَهُ بَنْفُولِيُو تَفَاصِيلَ الْحَادِثَةِ، وَكَيْفَ وَجَدَ خَادِمَيْهِمَا يَتَشَاجَرَانِ مَعَ خَادِمَيْ عَائِلَةِ كَابُولِيت فَأَرَادَ تَفْرِقَتَهُمَا، إِلَّا أَنَّ تَيْبَالْتَ حَالَ دُونَ ذَلِكَ وَاسْتَفَزَّهُ إِلَى أَنْ بَدَآ بِالشِّجَارِ هُمَا أَيْضًا، ثُمَّ كَيْفَ اجْتَمَعَ النَّاسُ شَيْئًا فَشَيْئًا.

أَمَّا السَّيِّدَةُ مُنْتِيغِيُو فَقَدْ بَدَتْ سَعِيدَةً؛ لِأَنَّ ابْنَهَا **رُومِيُو** لَمْ يَحْشُرْ نَفْسَهُ فِي الْمَعْرَكَةِ، إِلَّا أَنَّهَا أَعْرَبَتْ عَنْ قَلَقِهَا الشَّدِيدِ عَلَيْهِ فَسَأَلَتْ بَنْفُولِيُو عَنْ مَا إِذَا رَآهُ، فَرَدَّ قَائِلًا: "نَعَمْ سَيِّدَتِي! قَبْلَ فَجْرِ الْيَوْمِ كُنْتُ مَشْغُولًا وَأُفَكِّرُ كَثِيرًا، فَنَزَلْتُ أَتَمَشَّى وَهُنَالِكَ لَمَحْتُ ابْنَ عَمِّي رُومِيُو يَتَمَشَّى أَيْضًا... وَحِيدًا مِثْلِي. فَاتَّجَهْتُ صَوْبَهُ إِلَّا أَنَّهُ تَجَاهَلَنِي وَاخْتَفَى بَيْنَ أَشْجَارِ الْغَابَةِ. لَعَلَّهُ مِثْلِي تَمَامًا هَذِهِ الْأَيَّامِ؛ يُجِيدُ الْعُزْلَةَ وَلَا يَرْغَبُ فِي صُحْبَةِ أَحَدٍ..."

أَيَّدَهُ السَّيِّدُ مُنْتِيغِيُو قَائِلًا: "نَعَمْ، أَنْتَ عَلَى حَقٍّ يَا بَنْفُولِيُو! لَقَدْ شُوهِدَ ابْنِي رُومِيُو الْعَدِيدَ مِنَ الْمَرَّاتِ يَبْكِي وَحِيدًا، مُضِيفًا دُمُوعَهُ إِلَى

قَطَرَاتِ النَّدَى وَتَنَهُّدَاتِهِ إِلَى غُيُومِ السَّمَاءِ... ثُمَّ مَعَ بُزُوغِ الشَّمْسِ يَنْعَزِلُ فِي غُرْفَتِهِ هَارِبًا مِنَ النُّورِ... عَلَيْنَا أَنْ نَفْعَلَ شَيْئًا لِإِنْقَاذِهِ، وَإِلَّا فَسَيُصِيبُهُ مَكْرُوهٌ جَرَّاءَ مِزَاجِهِ الْمُتَشَائِمِ هَذَا! أَرْجُوكَ يَا بَنْفُولِيُو سَاعِدْهُ لِتَخَطِّي أَزْمَتِهِ الَّتِي لَا يَعْلَمُ أَسْبَابَهَا إِلَّا هُوَ..."

قَطَعَ بَنْفُولِيُو لِعَمِّهِ وَعْدًا أَنْ يُسَاعِدَ رُومْيُو وَيُنْقِذَهُ مِنَ اكْتِئَابِهِ.

وَفِعْلًا جَاوَلَ بَنْفُولِيُو جَاهِدًا إِخْرَاجَ رُومْيُو مِنْ صَمْتِهِ، إِلَى أَنْ نَجَحَ وَاسْتَدْرَجَهُ لِلْحَدِيثِ عَمَّا يَشْغُلُ أَفْكَارَهُ: "أَخْبِرْنِي رُومْيُو! مَا الَّذِي يَجْعَلُكَ تَعِيسًا كَئِيبًا هَكَذَا؟ صَارِحْنِي أَرْجُوكَ، هَلْ وَقَعْتَ فِي الْحُبِّ؟"

"وَقَعْتُ... بَلْ هَوَيْتُ... خَارِجَهُ"

"مَاذَا؟ خَارِجَهُ؟ مَاذَا تَعْنِي؟ وَقَعْتَ خَارِجَ الْحُبِّ؟"

"نَعَمْ... هُوَ حُبٌّ مِنْ طَرَفٍ وَاحِدٍ... أُحِبُّهَا وَلَكِنَّهَا لَا تُحِبُّنِي..."

شَعَرَ بَنْفُولِيُو بِالْحُزْنِ مِنْ أَجْلِ رُومْيُو، وَحَاوَلَ التَّرْفِيهَ عَنْهُ وَإِقْنَاعَهُ بِبَسَاطَةِ الْمَوْضُوعِ، مَعَ أَنَّ قَلْبَهُ كَادَ يَتَقَطَّعُ أَلَمًا عَلَيْهِ. سَأَلَهُ عَنِ اسْمِ

حَبيبَتِهِ، ولكِنَّ روميو رَفَضَ إِطْلاعَهُ عَلَيْها، إِلَّا أَنَّ بِنفوليو أَصَرَّ أَنْ يَعْرِفَ اسمَها:

"هَيَّا أَخْبِرْني أَرجوكَ! مَنْ تَكونُ هَذِهِ الَّتي سَلَبَتْكَ عَقْلَكَ؟"

وَبَعْدَ عَناءٍ طَويلٍ، باحَ روميو بِسِرِّهِ: "إِنَّها **روزالايْنْ** يا بِنفوليو! تِلكَ الفَتاةُ فائِقَةُ الجَمالِ وَالرِّقَّةِ، تِلكَ العَفيفَةُ الَّتي سَيَضيعُ جَمالُها هَدَرًا. لَنْ تَترُكَ أَحَدًا يَقتَرِبُ مِنها أَوْ يَنالُ مِنْ جَمالِها الفاتِنِ، فَقَدْ قَطَعَتْ عَلى نَفْسِها وَعْدًا أَنْ تَموتَ عَذراءَ، وَأَنْ لا تَسْقُطَ أَبَدًا في شِباكِ الحُبِّ... وهَذا ما جَعَلَني أَموتُ وَأَنا عَلى قَيْدِ الحَياةِ..."

ذَهِلَ بِنفوليو وَلَمْ يَجِدْ كَلامًا يُعَبِّرُ بِهِ عَنْ أَسَفِهِ عَلى ابنِ عَمِّهِ، إِلَّا أَنَّهُ سُرعانَ ما تَدارَكَ الأَمْرَ قائِلًا: "لا بَأْسَ روميو، خُذْ بِنَصيحَتي: لا تُفَكِّرْ بِها إِطْلاقًا! لِتَنْساها أَرْجوكَ..."

"عَلِّمْني كَيْفَ أَنْساها!"

"يَكْفي أَنْ تُطْلِقَ العِنانَ لِعَيْنَيْكَ وتَتَأَمَّلَ جَمالَ الفَتَياتِ اللَّاتي مِنْ حَوْلِكَ... وَسَوْفَ تَنْساها..."

بَدا روميو غَيْرَ مُقْتَنِعٍ بِكَلامِ بِنفوليو، وَأَخَذَ يَتَخَيَّلُ جَمالَ حَبيبَتِهِ

روزالاين... هِيَ الأَجْمَلُ بِالنِّسْبَةِ لَهُ، وَلَا يَتَصَوَّرُ أَبَدًا وُجُودَ فَتَيَاتٍ أَجْمَلَ مِنْهَا... إِنَّ فِكْرَةَ بِنْفُولِيو لَمْ تَزِدْهُ إِلَّا إِصْرَارًا عَلَى تَشَبُّثِهِ بِحُبِّ روزالاين. فَنَظَرَ بِيَأْسٍ إِلَى بِنْفُولِيو وَوَدَّعَهُ.

"سَأَجْعَلُكَ تَنْساها يا رومِيو! أَعِدُكَ! سَوْفَ تَنْساها..." صاحَ بِنْفُولِيو في حُزْنٍ.

في هذِهِ الأَثْناءِ، كانَ السَّيِّدُ كابوليت مُجْتَمِعًا في قَصْرِهِ بِالسَّيِّدِ باريس – أَحَدُ نُبَلاءِ الْبَلْدَةِ – يَتَحاوَرانِ حَوْلَ الْمَعْرَكَةِ الَّتِي نَشَبَتْ بَيْنَ أَفْرادِ عائِلَتِهِ وَعائِلَةِ مُنْتِيغْيو. عَبَّرَ السَّيِّدُ باريس عن اسْتِغْرابِهِ مِنْ تَوَتُّرِ الْعَلاقَةِ بَيْنَ الْعائِلَتَيْنِ، ثُمَّ سُرْعانَ ما غَيَّرَ الْمَوْضُوعَ لِيَتَطَرَّقَ إِلَى مَسْأَلَةِ زَواجِهِ بِابْنَةِ السَّيِّدِ كابوليت، وَالَّتِي كانَ قَدْ طَلَبَ مِنْهُ يَدَها، وَلَا يَزالُ يَنْتَظِرُ الْجَوابَ عَلَى أَحَرِّ مِنَ الْجَمْرِ. كانَ السَّيِّدُ كابوليت مُتَرَدِّدًا كَثِيرًا بِخُصُوصِ هذِهِ الْمَسْأَلَةِ، خاصَّةً وَأَنَّ ابْنَتَهُ لَمْ تَتَجاوَزِ الرّابِعَةَ عَشْرَةَ مِنْ عُمُرِها، إِلَّا أَنَّ باريس حاوَلَ إِقْناعَهُ بِأَنَّ هُناكَ مَنْ هُنَّ أَصْغَرُ سِنًّا مِنْها وَقَدْ تَزَوَّجْنَ وَهُنَّ سَعِيداتٌ جِدًّا بِزَواجِهِنَّ...

"اِجْعَلْها تُغْرَمُ بِكَ وَتَقَعُ في حُبِّكَ، فَأَنا لا أَسْتَطِيعُ إِجْبارَها عَلَى

حُبِّكَ! أنا مُوافِقٌ... وَلَكِنَّ القَرارَ الأَخيرَ يَعودُ إلَيْها... لِذَلِكَ تَعالَ اللَّيْلَةَ لِلسَّهْرَةِ الَّتي سَتُقامُ في قَصْرِنا... وَحاوِلِ التَّقَرُّبَ مِنْها، وَلَكِنَّني أُذَكِّرُكَ أَنَّكَ سَتَجِدُ العَديدَ مِنَ الجَميلاتِ هُنا، فَمِنَ المُحْتَمَلِ أَنْ تَنْسَى أَمْرَ ابْنَتي..." قالَ السَّيِّدُ كابوليت مُحاوِلًا إقْناعَ باريس بِالعُدولِ عَنْ فِكْرَةِ الزَّواجِ بِابْنَتِهِ.

في هَذِهِ الأَثْناءِ عَلِمَ روميو بِالسَّهْرَةِ الَّتي سَتُقامُ في مَنْزِلِ كابوليت، وَكَيْفَ لا وَحَبيبَتُهُ روزالاين مِنْ بَيْنِ المَدْعُوِّينَ؟! شَجَّعَهُ بنفوليو عَلى الذَّهابِ لِلحَفْلِ آمِلًا أَنْ تَعْتَرِضَ روميو جَميلاتٌ أُخْرَياتٌ تُنْسيهِ حُبَّ روزالاين، فَقَرَّرَ روميو الذَّهابَ، لَيْسَ مِنْ أَجْلِ الجَميلاتِ... بَلْ مِنْ أَجْلِ حَبيبَتِهِ روزالاين.

# Vocabulary

### p. 1

يُحْكَى أَنْ it is said that...
خِلافٌ dispute, hostility
حادٌّ sharp; heated, intense
نَشِبَ (نُشوبٌ) [1s4] to erupt, break out
نَبيلٌ (نُبلاءُ) noble; *elative* أَنْبَلُ
فيرونا Verona *(city)*
كابوليت Capulet *(family)*
مُنْتيغيو Montague *(family)*
عَريقٌ (عِراقٌ) respectable, of noble descent
عَداوَةٌ animosity
اِشْتَعَلَ [8s1] to burn, flare
نيرانٌ *f.* fire
صِراعٌ conflict
نُسِيَ (نِسْيانٌ/نَسْيٌ) [1d4] *pass.* to be forgotten

مَعَ مُرورِ الزَّمَنِ over time
كَراهِيَةٌ hatred
ظَلَّ مُتَواصِلًا (ظَلَّ) [1g1] to be continuous
وُرِثَ (وِرْثٌ/إِرْثٌ) [1a4] *pass.* to be inherited
جيلٌ (أَجْيالٌ) generation
سَمْبْسونْ Sampson *(name)*
تَجادَلَ مَعَ [6s] to argue with
غْريغوري Gregory *(name)*
وَسَطَ in the middle of
ساحَةٌ (عامَّةٌ) public square, plaza
عَدُوٌّ لَدودٌ (أَعْداءٌ لَدودونَ) archenemy

### p. 2

(خَدَمٌ) خادِمٌ servant
كُرْهٌ hate, hating
غَيْرُ مَسْبوقٍ unprecedented, unparalleled
مُتَشَنِّجٌ convulsive, jerky
عَصَبِيٌّ nervous

ضَيَّعَ [2s] to lose
اِسْتَفَزَّ [10g] to provoke
حَثَّ (حَثٌّ) [1g3] to urge
تَباهَى بِ [6d] to show off, boast
مَهارَةٌ (مَهاراتٌ) skill

قِتالِيٌّ fighting-, combatant
فَتَكَ بِ (فَتْكٌ) [1s2] to slay, ravage
رَفَقَ بِ (رِفْقٌ) [1s3] to be lenient toward
قَتَلَ (قَتْلٌ) [1s3] to kill
رَقِيقٌ (رِقاقٌ) tender, gentle
مُهَذَّبٌ polite
سَلَبَ (سَلْبٌ) [1s3] to deprive of, strip of; to loot, rob
عُذْرَةٌ (عُذْرٌ) virginity
صاحَ (صِياحٌ) [1h2] to shout
تَوَعَّدَ [5s] to threaten
اِزْدادَ [8h1] to increase, grow
حَماسٌ enthusiasm
شَرَعَ في (شُروعٌ) [1s1] to start to
تَوَعُّدٌ bluster, threatening talk
هَدَّدَ (تَهْدِيدٌ) [2s] to threaten
لَمَحَ (لَمْحٌ) [1s1] to spot, notice
أَبْراهام Abraham, Abram (name)
بِرِفْقَةِ accompanied by
اِقْتَرَبَ مِنْ [8s1] to approach, come near

شَيْئًا فَشَيْئًا gradually, little, by little
ظَهَرَ (ظُهورٌ) [1s1] to appear
قَلَقٌ concern, worry, anxiety
وَجْهٌ (وُجوهٌ) face
في حينِ while
واصَلَ [3s] to continue
لَهْجَةٌ tone, style of speaking
مُتَحَدِّيٌ defiant
إلّا أنّ but, however
قانونٌ (قَوانينُ) law, rule
شِجارٌ (شُجُرٌ) fight, quarrel
حَمى (حِمايَةٌ) [1d2] to defend, protect
قَضَمَ (قَضْمٌ) [1s2] to bite, nibble (Biting down on your thumb was an obscene gesture in Shakespeare's time, similar to extending a middle finger nowadays.)
إصْبَعٌ (أصابِعُ) finger
لا أَخْلاقِيٌّ vulgar, unethical

p. 3

غَضَبٌ anger
عَيْنٌ (أَعْيُنٌ) eye
قَصَدَ (قَصْدٌ) [1s2] to mean, intend; to head for
إهانَةٌ insult
رَفيقٌ (رِفاقٌ) companion
نَفى (نَفْيٌ) [1d2] to deny

قامَ بِ (قِيامٌ) [1h3] to perform, do
تَدَخَّلَ [5s] to intervene
اِتَّهَمَ بِ [8a1] to accuse of
حاوَلَ (مُحاوَلَةٌ) [3s] to attempt, try
نَجَحَ في (نَجاحٌ) [1s1] to succeed in
سَلَّ (سَلٌّ) [1g3] to draw, unsheathe

سَيْفٌ (سُيوفٌ) sword
تَشاجَرَ [6s] to fight
بَنْفولْيو Benvolio (name)
قَريبٌ (أَقْرِباءُ) relative
بِدَوْرِهِ in turn
صَرَخَ (صُراخٌ) [1s3] to shout, cry
فَوْرًا immediately
أَيُّها o (vocative)
غَبِيٌّ (أَغْبِياءُ) fool, idiot; stupid, foolish
هَيّا come on
أَلْقى [4d] to throw down, discard
حالًا immediately
مَدى extent
خُطورَةٌ gravity, seriousness
دَعْكَ مِنْ imperative leave (be)!
نِدًّا لِنِدٍّ peer to peer, as equals

جُرْأَةٌ boldness, courage
اِلْتَفَتَ [8s1] to turn (around)
وَجَدَ (وُجودٌ) [1a2] to find
تَيْبالْت Tybalt (name)
مَشْهورٌ (مَشاهيرُ) famous
غَطْرَسَةٌ arrogance
عِنادٌ stubbornness
أَقْنَعَ بِ (إِقْناعٌ) [4s] to persuade, convince (of)
سِلْمٌ (أَسْلُمٌ) peace
هُدوءٌ calm
اِسْتَهْزَأَ [10s(c)] to mock, laugh scornfully at
أَشْهَرَ [4s] to brandish; make public
سِلاحٌ (أَسْلِحَةٌ) weapon, arms

*p. 4*

كَرِهَ (كُرْهٌ/كَرْهٌ) [1s4] to hate
قاتَلَ [3s] to combat, fight against
جَبانٌ (جُبَناءُ) coward
اِحْتَشَدَ [8s1] to gather, rally
جَماهيرُ pl. crowd, masses
هَتَفَ (هُتافٌ) [1s2] to call out, shout
شَجَّعَ (تَشْجيعٌ) [2s] to encourage
تارَةً... وَتارَةً sometimes ... and sometimes
هَرَعَ (هَرَعٌ) [1s1] to hurry, rush
اِكْتَشَفَ (اِكْتِشافٌ) [8s1] to discover

اِنْدَفَعَ [7s] to rush, charge
بَرْقٌ (بُروقٌ) lightning
اِنْضَمَّ إِلى (اِنْضِمامٌ) [7g] to join
مَعْرَكَةٌ (مَعارِكُ) battle
هَدَّأَ (تَهْدِئَةٌ) [2s(c)] to calm
أَجْواءٌ pl. atmosphere
فَجْأَةً suddenly
أَميرٌ (أُمَراءُ) prince
أَسْكاليس Escalus (name)
تَطايَرَ [6s] to emanate, disperse
خاطَبَ [3s] to address
رَعِيَّةٌ (رَعايا) subjects; flock
مُتَمَرِّدٌ rebel

تَجَرَّأَ [5s(c)] to dare
سِوَى except, besides
وَحْشٌ (وُحُوشٌ) beast, monster
ضَارِيٌ savage, ferocious
شَاهَدَ (مُشَاهَدَةٌ) [3s] to watch, observe
سَالَ (سَيَلَانٌ) [1h2] to flow
دَمٌ (دِمَاءٌ) blood
بَعْضُهُمُ الْبَعْضَ each other
أَمْنٌ security, safety

شَهِدَ (شَهَادَةٌ) [1s4] to witness, testify
فَوْضَى chaos, anarchy
عَارِمٌ (عُرَّمٌ) overwhelming, tremendous
كَفَاكَ + indefinite accusative masdar stop...!
اِمْتَثَلَ لِ (اِمْتِثَالٌ) [8s1] to obey
عَاقِبَةٌ (عَوَاقِبُ) consequence
عَذَّبَ (تَعْذِيبٌ) [2s] to torture

*p. 5*

أَمْرٌ (أَوَامِرُ) command, order
غَاضِبٌ angry
هَدَأَ (هُدُوءٌ) [1s1(b)] to calm down
اِنْسَحَبَ [7s] to withdraw
بَقِيَ (بَقَاءٌ) [1d4] to stay
سَيِّدٌ (سَادَةٌ) master, lord
قَلِقٌ worried, anxious
بِشَأْنِ about, regarding
حَدَثَ (حُدُوثٌ) [1s3] to happen
سَرَدَ لِ (سَرْدٌ) [1s3] to recount, report to; to enumerate, list
تَفَاصِيلُ (تَفَاصِيلُ) detail
حَادِثَةٌ (حَوَادِثُ) incident
فَرَّقَ (تَفْرِقَةٌ) [2s] to separate
حَالَ دُونَ (حَيْلُولَةٌ) [1h3] to prevent
سَيِّدَةٌ lady
رُومِيُو Romeo (name)
حَشَرَ نَفْسَهُ فِي (حَشْرٌ) [1s3] to get caught up in
أَعْرَبَ [4s] to express

فَجْرٌ dawn
تَمَشَّى [5d] to stroll, go for a walk
اِتَّجَهَ صَوْبَ [8a1] to head toward
تَجَاهَلَ [6s] to ignore
اِخْتَفَى [8d1] to disappear
غَابَةٌ forest
لَعَلَّ + suffixed pronoun perhaps
حَبَّذَ [2s] to favor
عُزْلَةٌ solitude, isolation
رَغِبَ (رَغْبَةٌ) [1s4] to wish, desire
صُحْبَةٌ companionship: /
فِي صُحْبَةِ accompanied by
أَيَّدَ (تَأْيِيدٌ) [2s(a)] to concur, affirm
كَانَ عَلَى حَقٍّ (كَوْنٌ) [1h3] to be right
شُوهِدَ [3s] *pass.* to be seen / observed
بَكَى (بُكَاءٌ) [1d2] to cry
مُضِيفٌ إِضَافَةٌ adding: [4h] to add
دَمْعَةٌ (دُمُوعٌ) tear

## p. 6

قَطَرةٌ drop
(أَنْداءٌ) نَدًى dew
[5s] (تَنَهُّدْ) تَنَهَّدَ to sigh
غُيومٌ *pl.* clouds
مَعَ بُزوغِ (أَبْزِغَةٌ) بُزوغٌ emergence:
الشَّمْسِ at the crack of dawn
[7s] اِنْعَزَلَ to confine onself, withdraw
(هُروبٌ/هَرَبٌ) هَرَبَ [1s3] to escape
(إِنْقاذٌ) أَنْقَذَ [4s] to rescue, save
أَصابَ [4h] to afflict, befall
مَكْروهٌ ordeal, disasster
جَرّاءَ as a result of, because of
(أَمْزِجَةٌ) مِزاجٌ mood
مُتَشائِمٌ pessimistic
أَرْجوكَ please, I beg you
(تَخَطٍّ) تَخَطَّى [5d] to overcome, exceed
أَزْمَةٌ crisis
(قَطْعٌ) قَطَعَ لِ وَعْدًا [1s1] to make a promise to
اِكْتِئابٌ depression
حاوَلَ جاهِدًا [3s] to try hard

(إِخْراجٌ) أَخْرَجَ [4s] to bring out, extract
صَمْتٌ silence
اِسْتَدْرَجَ [10s] to lure, entice gradually
(أَحاديثُ) حَديثٌ conversation, discourse
(شُغْلٌ) شَغَلَ [1s1] to occupy, make busy
(جَعْلٌ) جَعَلَ [1s1] to cause, make
(تُعَساءُ) تَعيسٌ miserable, poor
كَئيبٌ bleak
صارَحَ [3s] to speak frankly
(هُوِيٌّ) هَوَى [1d2] to collapse
خارِجَ outside of
(أَطْرافٌ) طَرَفٌ side
(أَحْزانٌ) حُزْنٌ sadness, sorrow
مِنْ أَجْلِ for, for the sake of
(تَرْفِيَةٌ) رَفَّهَ عَنْ [2s] to cheer up
بَساطَةٌ simplicity
(كَيْدٌ) كادَ [1h1] + *indicative* to almost (do); to be about to
تَقَطَّعَ [5s] to break (apart)

## p. 7

(رَفْضٌ) رَفَضَ [1s2] to refuse, decline
(إِطْلاعٌ) أَطْلَعَ عَلى [4s] to inform, let know about
(إِضْرارٌ) أَصَرَّ [4g] to insist

(عُقولٌ) عَقْلٌ mind
عَناءٌ trouble, effort
باحَ [1h3] to divulge, disclose
(أَسْرارٌ) سِرٌّ secret
روزالاين Rosaline *(name)*

فائِقٌ + *noun* extensive, considerable
رِقَّةٌ tenderness, softness
عَفيفٌ celibate, chaste
هَدَرًا in vain, wasted
نالَ مِنْ (نَيْلٌ/مَنالٌ) [1h1] to gain, win
فاتِنٌ alluring, charming
عَذْراءُ (عَذارَى) virgin, maiden
سَقَطَ في شِباكِ الحُبِّ (سُقوطٌ) [1s3] to fall in love
عَلى قَيْدِ الحَياةِ alive
ذَهِلَ (ذُهولٌ) [1s4] to be astounded

تَصَوَّرَ [5s] to imagine, picture
تَشَبُّثٌ بِ attachment to
بِيَأْسٍ desperately
وَدَّعَ [2s] to say goodbye (to), bid farewell
قَصْرٌ (قُصورٌ) palace
باريس Paris (*name*)
تَحاوَرَ حَوْلَ [6s] to discuss, talk about
اِسْتَغْرَبَ (اِسْتِغْرابٌ) [10s] to find unusual
تَوَتُّرٌ tension
تَطَرَّقَ إلى [5s] to address, deal with

عَبَّرَ (بِ) عَنْ [2s] to express (with)
سُرْعانَ ما quickly, soon
تَدارَكَ [6s] to rectify, correct
لا بَأْسَ it's all right, never mind
نَصيحَةٌ (نَصائِحُ) advice, tip
إِطْلاقًا (not) at all
أَطْلَقَ العِنانَ لِ [4s] to unleash, release
تَأَمَّلَ [5s(a)] to contemplate, meditate on
مِنْ حَوْلِ around, surrounding
اِقْتَنَعَ بِ (اِقْتِناعٌ) [8s2] to be convinced of
تَخَيَّلَ [5s] to imagine, picture

*p. 8*

زَواجٌ marriage
لا يَزالُ still (does)
اِنْتَظَرَ (اِنْتِظارٌ) [8s1] to wait
عَلى أَحَرَّ مِنَ الجَمْرِ on pins and needles
مُتَرَدِّدٌ hesitant
بِخُصوصِ concerning, regarding
خاصَّةً especially
تَجاوَزَ [6s] to be past (an age)
تَزَوَّجَ (تَزَوُّجٌ) [5s] to get married
أُغْرِمَ بِ [4s] *pass.* to be in love with
أَجْبَرَ عَلى (إِجْبارٌ) [4s] to coerce, force

*p. 9*

مُوافِقٌ approving
سَهْرَةٌ party
(تَقَرُّبٌ) تَقَرَّبَ مِن [5s] to get closer to, approach
جَمِيلَةٌ beauty, lovely lady
مِنَ الْمُحْتَمَلِ أَنْ probably, likely
(عُدولٌ) عَدَلَ مِنْ [1s2] to dissuade from

مَدْعُوٌّ invited, invitee
حَفْلٌ ball, gala
(آمَلٌ) أَمَلَ [1s3(a)] to hope
اِعْتَرَضَ [8s] to object, take exception to
حَسْناءُ (حَسْناواتٌ) beauty, belle, lovely lady
أَنْسَى [4s] to make forget

## Translation

*p. 1*

It is said that a heated dispute broke out between two of the noblest families in the Italian city of Verona, the Capulet family and the Montague family–two highborn families united by an animosity that had been burning for so many years that the causes of conflict between them had been forgotten over time, but their hatred continued as if inherited from generation to generation.

Sampson seemed to be arguing with Gregory in the middle of a public square in Verona, but in fact, they were talking about their archenemies, the Montague family!

*p. 2*

Sampson and Gregory were servants of the Capulet family. An unparalleled hatred of the Montague family united them.

Sampson was jerky and nervous, so Gregory was not going to waste an opportunity to provoke him and urge him to show off his strength and combat skills with which he would slay the members of the Montague family.

"I will have no mercy on their men... I will kill them all! And the women, I will be gentle and polite with them... I will steal their virginity!" Sampson shouted threateningly.

The more Gregory provoked him, the more his enthusiasm grew as he started to bluster and make threats. They went on like this until they spotted Abraham, accompanied by another servant of the Montague family, coming from afar and gradually approaching them.

Worry appeared on Gregory's face, while Sampson continued in his defiant tone, but he did not want to break the law this time. He looked at Gregory saying, "The law has to be on our side! It must be they who start the fighting; that way the law will protect us."

Sampson bit his [own] finger in a provocative, vulgar gesture. Abraham asked him, ...

*p. 3*

with anger in his eyes whether he intended to insult him and his companion with his gesture. Sampson replied in denial, "No, I did not mean it for you... but I did, in fact, make an obscene gesture."

Then Gregory intervened, accusing Abraham of trying to start a fight. And he succeeded, indeed, in provoking the servants of the Capulet family. Everyone drew their swords and began to fight.

Meanwhile, Benvolio, a relative of the Montague family, arrived and, in turn, drew his sword, shouting at them, "Stop this fighting immediately, you fools! Come now, throw your swords down immediately! You do not know how dangerous what you are doing is!"

"Benvolio! Leave these servants be and come fight peer to peer. Do you have the courage?"

Benvolio turned to see who was talking to him and found Tybalt, a relative of the Capulet family, who was famous for his arrogance and stubbornness. He tried to convince him of peace and calm, but Tybalt answered him mockingly,

"What peace are you talking about? And what quiet are you talking about? You brandish your weapon, then...

*p. 4*

you talk about peace? Peace... How I hate this word, and how I hate the Montague family and you along with them! Come on, fight me, coward! Come!"

They began to fight, and a crowd gathered, cheering and encouraging at times Benvolio and at times Tybalt, sometimes calling out the name "Capulet" and sometimes the name "Montague"... until Lord Capulet and Lord Montague, accompanied by their wives, hurried to the scene to find out the reason for the gathering and the shouting.

The two men rushed at lightning speed to join the fight, while their wives were trying to calm the atmosphere.

Suddenly, the prince of the town, Escalus, appeared with his men. Anger seemed to be flying out of his eyes, and he shouted, addressing his subjects, "You rebels! Enemies of peace! You who dare to brandish weapons in his neighbor's face! You are nothing but savage beasts who enjoy watching each other's blood flow! This is the third time that my city has been in turmoil because of the quarrels between the Capulets and Montagues. Stop fighting! You will obey me immediately and throw down your weapons. Otherwise, the consequence for you is to be tortured to death."

*p. 5*

They all threw their weapons on the ground as fear appeared on their faces, obeying the orders of their angry prince. The atmosphere calmed down and everyone retreated from the square. Only Lord Montague, his wife, and Benvolio remained.

Lord Montague was worried about what had happened. Benvolio told him the details of the incident and how they found their servants fighting with the

Capulet servants, so he wanted to separate them, but Tybalt prevented it and provoked him until they too started fighting, and then people gradually gathered around.

Lady Montague looked happy because her son Romeo had not gotten caught up in the fight, but she was very concerned about him. She asked Benvolio whether he had seen him. He replied, "Yes, madam! Before dawn today, I was busy thinking a lot, so I went out for a walk, and there I caught sight of my cousin Romeo walking, too... alone like me. I turned towards him, but he ignored me and disappeared among the trees of the forest. Perhaps he is just like me these days, preferring to be alone and not desiring to be in the company of anyone."

Lord Montague concurred with him, "Yes, you are right, Benvolio! My son Romeo has been seen many times weeping alone, adding his tears to...

*p. 6*

dew drops and his sighs to the clouds of the sky. Then, with the rising of the sun, he withdraws to his room, fleeing the light. We have to do something to save him; otherwise, a misfortune would befall him because of this pessimistic mood of his! Please, Benvolio, help him to overcome his crisis, the causes of which only he knows."

Benvolio made his uncle a promise to help Romeo and save him from his depression.

૭ ૭ ૭

Indeed, Benvolio tried hard to bring Romeo out of his silence until he managed to get him to talk about his thoughts. "Tell me, Romeo, what makes you miserable like this? Please, tell me, have you fallen in love?"

"I have fallen... I have collapsed... out of it."

"What? Out of it? What do you mean? You've fallen out

of love?"

"Yes… it's love from one side. I love her, but she does not love me."

Benvolio felt sad for Romeo and tried to comfort him and to convince him of the simplicity of the matter, even though his heart was breaking for him. He asked him about his love's name,…

*p. 7*

but Romeo refused to let him know. However, Benvolio insisted on knowing her name.

"Come on, tell me, please! Who is this [woman] who has robbed your mind?

After a long effort, Romeo revealed his secret. "It's Rosaline, Benvolio! That girl of beauty and tenderness, the chaste one whose beauty will be wasted. She will not let anyone approach her or win her alluring beauty. She has promised herself to die a virgin and that she will never fall in love. And this is what made me die although I'm still alive."

Benvolio was stunned and did not find any words to express regret for his cousin, but he quickly corrected the matter saying, "It's all right, Romeo. Take my advice: Do not think about it at all! Forget her, I beg you."

"Teach me how to forget her!"

"It's enough to unleash your eyes and contemplate the beauty of the girls around you… and you will forget her."

Romeo seemed unconvinced by Benvolio's words. He imagined the beauty of his beloved Rosaline…

*p. 8*

She was the most beautiful to him, and he couldn't imagine that more beautiful girls could exist. Benvolio's idea only reinforced his insistence on his attachment to Rosaline. He looked desperately at Benvolio and bid him farewell.

"I will make you forget her, Romeo! I promise you, you will forget her," Benvolio cried in sorrow.

Meanwhile, Lord Capulet was meeting at his palace with Lord Paris, a nobleman in the town, discussing the feud between his family and the Montague family. Lord Paris expressed surprise at the tension between the two families and quickly changed the subject to address the issue of his marriage to the daughter of Lord Capulet, whose hand he had asked for. He was still waiting for the answer on pins and needles. Lord Capulet was very hesitant about this issue, especially since his daughter was only 14 years old, but Paris tried to convince him that some younger than her had married and were happy in their marriages.

"Make her love you, for I cannot force her to...

*p. 9*

love you. I approve, but the final decision rests on her. So, come tonight for a party at our palace. Try to get closer to her, but I remind you that you will find many beautiful women here, you may forget the matter about my daughter," Lord Capulet said, trying to persuade Paris to abandon the idea of marrying his daughter.

In the meantime, Romeo learned of the party that would be held at the Capulet's residence. And how would he not, when his love, Rosaline, was among the invitees?! Benvolio encouraged him to go to the party in the hope that Romeo would meet other beautiful women that would make him forget about his love for Rosaline. Romeo decided to go, not for the beautiful women, but for his beloved Rosaline.

# اَلْفَصْلُ الثَّاني

بَيْنما كانَ الْخَدَمُ مَشْغولينَ بِإِعْدادِ السَّهْرَةِ، وَتَنْظيمِ الْمَوائِدِ في مَنْزِلِ كابوليتْ، كانَتِ السَّيِّدَةُ كابوليتْ مُجْتَمِعَةً بِابْنَتِها **جولييتْ** وَبِالْمُرَبِّيَةِ في إِحْدى الْغُرَفِ، يَتَجاذَبْنَ أَطْرافَ الْحَديثِ.

بَدَأَتِ الْمُرَبِّيَةُ تَتَذَكَّرُ أَيَّامَ طُفولَةِ جولييتْ وَغَرِقَتْ في الْحَديثِ عَنْ تِلْكَ الْأَيَّامِ، مُتَماديَةً في الْمُزاحِ، وَسَرْدِ نُكَتٍ سَخيفَةٍ وَسافِلَةٍ، مِمَّا أَثارَ غَضَبَ جولييتْ وَوالِدَتِها فَسُرْعانَ ما غَيَّرَتِ السَّيِّدَةُ كابوليتْ الْحَديثَ لِتَتَطَرَّقَ إِلى مَوْضوعٍ أَكْثَرَ أَهَمِّيَّةً وَجِدِّيَّةً، أَلا وَهُوَ عُمْرُ جولييتْ وَمَدى اسْتِعْدادِها لِلزَّواجِ.

كانَتِ السَّيِّدَةُ كابوليت تُحاوِلُ جاهِدَةً إقْناعَ ابْنَتِها الَّتي لَمْ تَبْلُغْ بَعْدُ الرَّابِعَةَ عَشَرَةَ مِنْ عُمْرِها بِفِكْرَةِ الزَّواجِ باكِرًا، مُشيرَةً إلَى أنَّ العَديدَ مِنْ فَتَياتِ فيرونا قَدْ تَزَوَّجْنَ صِغارَ السِّنِّ، وَهُنَّ سعيداتٌ بِزواجِهنَّ.

وسُرْعانَ ما أَفْصَحَتْ لَها: "سَأَخْتَصِرُ لَكِ حَديثي يا ابْنَتي، إنَّ السَّيِّدَ باريس، ذَلِكَ الشَّابُّ الشَّهْمُ الْباسِلُ، يُريدُكِ زَوْجَةً لَهُ..."

"وَيا لَهُ مِنْ رَجُلٍ! إنَّهُ لَحَقًّا رَجُلٌ عَظيمٌ..." قاطَعَتْها الْمُرَبِّيَةُ مُتَحَمِّسَةً.

وَاصَلَتِ السَّيِّدَةُ كابوليت تَعُدُّ وَتُحْصي خِصالَ وَمُميزاتِ باريس وَخاصَّةً أَمْلاكَهُ مُحاوِلَةً لَفْتَ انْتِباهِ جولييت، وَخَتَمَتْ مَدْحَهُ بِإخْبارِ ابْنَتِها أنَّهُ آتٍ لِلسَّهْرَةِ الَّتي أَعَدَّها والِدُها.

بَدَأَتْ جولييت تَقْتَنِعُ قَليلًا بِكَلامِ والِدَتِها وَمُرَبِّيَتِها وَوَعَدَتْهُما أَنْ تُحاوِلَ أَنْ تُعْجَبَ بِهِ خِلالَ السَّهْرَةِ.

وَبَيْنَما هُنَّ يَتَجاذَبْنَ أَطْرافَ الْحَديثِ، دَخَلَ عَلَيْهِنَّ بيتْرْ – خادِمُ عائِلَةِ كابوليت – وَقاطَعَهُنَّ، مُخاطِبًا السَّيِّدَةَ كابوليت: "سَيِّدَتي، الْعَشاءُ جاهِزٌ وَالضُّيوفُ قَدْ أَتَوْا ويَنْتَظِرونَكِ... وَهُمْ مُتَشَوِّقونَ لِرُؤْيَةِ

آنِسَتي جوليِيت. هَيَّا لِنَلْتَحِقَ بِهِمْ قَبْلَ أَنْ يَنْفَذَ صَبْرُهُمْ."

"هَيَّا يا جوليِيت، أَسْرِعي!" صاحَتِ السَّيِّدَةُ كابوليت.

※

في هَذِهِ الأَثْناءِ، دَخَلَ روميو صُحْبَةَ ابْنَ عَمِّهِ بنفوليو وَصَديقِهِما مَرْكوشيو إلى قَصْرِ كابوليت مُتَنَكِّرينَ بِأَقْنِعَةٍ كَيْ لا يَتَفَطَّنَ لِوُجودِهِم أَحَدٌ، وَكانَ بِرِفْقَتِهِم خَمْسُ أَوْ سِتُّ رِجالٍ مُتَنَكِّرينَ أَيْضًا وَحامِلينَ مَشاعِلَ في أَيديهِم. بَدا روميو مُتَوَتِّرًا قَليلًا، إلَّا أَنَّ بنفوليو طَمْأَنَهُ وَوَعَدَهُ أَنْ يَرْقُصوا قَليلًا وَيَسْتَمْتِعوا بِالسَّهْرَةِ ثُمَّ يَعودونَ أَدْراجَهُمْ إلى الْمَنْزِلِ.

"لا يا بنفوليو" أَجابَهُ روميو في حُزْنٍ "إنّي أَشْعُرُ بِالْحُزْنِ... وَلَيْسَ لَدَيَّ أَيُّ رَغْبَةٍ في الرَّقْصِ، أَعْطِني ذَلِكَ الْمَشْعَلَ وَاذْهَبْ أَنْتَ لِلرَّقْصِ."

"لا يا صَديقي الْعَزيزُ" رَدَّ عَلَيْهِ مَرْكوشيو "أَنْتَ مُجْبَرٌ عَلَى الرَّقْصِ وَسَتَرْقُصُ، فَأَنْتَ مُغْرَمٌ وَبِالتَّالي عَلَيْكَ أَنْ تَسْعَدَ وَتَبْتَهِجَ وَتَرْقُصَ، فَالْحُبُّ إحْساسٌ جَميلٌ وَرَقيقٌ يَسْتَحِقُّ السَّعادَةَ!"

"أَحَقًّا؟ بَلْ قُلْ هُوَ عَنِيفٌ وَفَظٌّ وَقَاسٍ،" أَجَابَهُ رُومِيُو بِحَسْرَةٍ.

"حَسَنًا، حَسَنًا، إِنْ كَانَ الْحُبُّ هَكَذَا فَعَلَيْكَ أَنْ تَكُونَ عَنِيفًا مَعَهُ أَنْتَ أَيْضًا وَسَتَنْتَصِرُ عَلَيْهِ حَتْمًا!"

وَكَالْعَادَةِ، لَمْ يَقْتَنِعْ رُومِيُو بِكَلَامِ مَرْكُوشْيُو، فِي حِينِ كَانَ هَذَا الْأَخِيرُ مُصَمِّمًا أَنْ يُخْرِجَ رُومِيُو مِنْ حُزْنِهِ وَتَعَاسَتِهِ.

أَمَّا رُومِيُو، فَخَتَمَ تَشَاؤُمَهُ قَائِلًا: "عَلَى كُلٍّ، أَنَا أَشْعُرُ أَنَّ حَفْلَةَ اللَّيْلَةِ سَتَكُونُ بِدَايَةً لِمَكْرُوهٍ مَا قَدْ يُصِيبُنِي... لِحَدِيثٍ أَوْ لِطَارِئٍ سَيَنْتَهِي بِنِهَايَتِي... وَلَكِنْ... لَا عَلَيْنَا، لِيَلْعَبْ الْقَدَرُ لُعْبَتَهُ! هَيَّا بِنَا إِلَى الدَّاخِلِ يَا شَبَابُ!"

كَانَ الضُّيُوفُ مُجْتَمِعِينَ فِي قَصْرِ كَابُولِيتْ يَتَبَادَلُونَ أَطْرَافَ الْحَدِيثِ وَيَتَسَامَرُونَ، يَشْرَبُونَ وَيَأْكُلُونَ. وَقَفَ السَّيِّدُ كَابُولِيتْ وَسْطَهُمْ وَأَلْقَى خِطَابًا قَصِيرًا فِي الْمَدْعُوِّينَ مُرَحِّبًا بِهِمْ: "أَهْلًا وَسَهْلًا بِكُمْ ضُيُوفِي الْأَعِزَّاءِ... هَيَّا لِتَسْتَمْتِعُوا بِالسَّهْرَةِ، أَرْقُصُوا... فَأَنَا قَدْ هَرِمْتُ لِأَرْقُصَ مِثْلَكُمْ... فَارْقُصُوا أَنْتُمْ بَدَلِي. وَأَنْتُمْ أَيُّهَا الْمُوسِيقِيُّونَ! الْعَبُوا عَلَى

آلاتِكُمْ وَأَمْتِعونا بِموسيقاكُمْ... مَرْحَبًا بِالْجَميعِ! سَهْرَةً طَيِّبَةً!"

بَدَأَ الْجَميعُ بِالرَّقْصِ، أَمَّا روميو فَوَقَفَ بَعيدًا يَتَأَمَّلُ في الْحاضِرينَ وَرُبَّما كانَ يَبْحَثُ عَنْ حَبيبَتِهِ روزالاينْ، مَنْ يَدْري؟ ...

فَإِذا بِهِ يَلْمَحُ فَتاةً فاقَ جَمالُها بِخَيالَهُ، وَضاهَتْ رِقَّتُها رِقَّةَ طَيْرِ الْيَمامِ، حَتَّى بَدَتْ لَهُ وَكَأَنَّها يَمامَةٌ وَسَطَ سِرْبٍ مِنَ الْغِرْبانِ. وَقَفَ في ذُهولٍ يَتَأَمَّلُها وَيُراقِبُ حَرَكاتِها وَكَأَنَّهُ مَسْحورٌ وَسَأَلَ نَفْسَهُ: "هَلْ أَنا مُتَأَكِّدٌ أَنَّ قَلْبي قَدْ خَفَقَ حَقًّا قَبْلَ هَذِهِ الْمَرَّةِ؟ لا! لا أَظُنُّ! لا شَكَّ أَنَّ عَيْنايَ كاذِبَتانِ، فَهَذِهِ أَوَّلُ مَرَّةٍ أَرى فيها جَمالًا حَقيقِيًّا!"

وَبَيْنَما كانَ روميو مُنْبَهِرًا بِجَمالِ الْفَتاةِ، تَفَطَّنَ لِوُجودِهِ تَيْبالْتْ، اِبْنَ عَمِّها؛ فَاسْتَشاطَ غَضَبًا وَسُرْعانَ ما أَحْكَمَ قَبْضَتَهُ عَلى سِلاحِهِ وَهَمَّ بِاتِّجاهِ روميو يَصْرُخُ وَيَتَوَعَّدُ. فَتَوَقَّفَ الْجَميعُ عَنِ الرَّقْصِ.

هُنا، تَدَخَّلَ عَمُّ تَيْبالْتْ، السَّيِّدُ كابوليتْ، وَحاوَلَ تَهْدِئَتَهُ قائِلًا: "أَرْجوكَ اِهْدَأْ يا بُنَيَّ، فَما الْعَيْبُ في حُضورِهِ؟ كَما أَنَّهُ مَشْهورٌ في كامِلِ أَرْجاءِ فيرونا بِشَهامَتِهِ وَبِأَخْلاقِهِ النَّبيلَةِ... فَاتْرُكْهُ وَشَأْنَهُ! أَرْجوكَ ...فَأَنا لا أَسْتَطيعُ طَرْدَهُ مِنْ مَنْزِلي!"

إِلَّا أَنَّ هذا لَمْ يَزِدْ إِلَّا تَجْرِيضًا في نَفْسِ تَيْبالْتَ وَعِنادًا، مِمَّا أَثارَ غَضَبَ السَّيِّدِ كابوليت، فَأُطْرِدَ تَيْبالْتَ مِنَ الْحَفْلَةِ أَمامَ مَرْأى الْجَمِيعِ. اِمْتَثَلَ تَيْبالْتَ لِأَوامِرِ عَمِّهِ وَخَرَجَ مِنَ الْقاعَةِ مُتَوَعِّدًا روميو وَالْجَمِيعُ يَنْظُرُ إِلَيْهِ.

"هَيَّا عودوا إِلَى الرَّقْصِ! اِسْتَمْتِعوا بِسَهْرَتِكُمْ أَيُّها الضُّيوفُ الْكِرامُ!" هَتَفَ السَّيِّدُ كابوليت في الْحاضِرينَ، فَعادَ الْجَميعُ إِلَى الرَّقْصِ وَالْغِناءِ.

اِسْتَغَلَّ روميو الْفُرْصَةَ لِيَقْتَرِبَ مِنَ الْجَميلَةِ الَّتي سَلَبَتْ عَقْلَهُ وَيُمْسِكَ بِيَدِها مُنْبَهِرًا بِرِقَّةِ مَلْمَسِها. بَدَتْ هِيَ أَيْضًا مُعْجَبَةً بِهِ... فَهُوَ حَقًّا شابٌ وَسيمٌ جِدًّا! أَطْلَقَتِ الْعِنانَ لِخَيالِها مُفَكِّرَةً بِهِ وَبِوَسامَتِهِ.

وَفَجْأَةً، غافَلَها روميو مُحاوِلًا تَقْبيلَها إِلَّا أَنَّها فَزِعَتْ وَاِمْتَنَعَتْ خَجَلًا. فَظَلَّ يُغازِلُها مَفْتونًا بِحُسْنِها وَبِرِقَّتِها... وَاِخْتَطَفَ قُبْلَةً سَريعَةً مِن شِفَتَيْها. اِحْمَرَّتْ وَجْنَتا جولييت خَجَلًا وَلكِنَّها وَقَعَتْ في حُبِّ روميو وَأُعْجِبَتْ بِقُبْلَتِهِ فَقَبَّلَتْهُ وَقَلْبُها يَخْفِقُ وَعَيْناها لا تُفارِقانِ عَيْنَيْهِ...

وَكانَ الْحُبُّ مِنَ النَّظْرَةِ الْأولى!

ظَلَّا يَتَبَادَلَانِ نَظَرَاتِ الْحُبِّ وَالْإِعْجَابِ فِي صَمْتٍ إِلَى أَنْ قَاطَعَتْهُمَا الْمُرَبِّيَةُ: "آنِسَتِي! وَالِدَتُكِ تُرِيدُكِ حَالًا!"

"وَمَنْ تَكُونُ وَالِدَتُهَا؟" تَسَاءَلَ رُومِيُو.

"وَالِدَتُهَا هِيَ سَيِّدَةُ هَذَا الْمَنْزِلِ! سَيِّدَةٌ عَظِيمَةٌ وَفَاضِلَةٌ. أَنَا الَّتِي قُمْتُ بِتَرْبِيَةِ ابْنَتِهَا... جُولِييت، تِلْكَ الْآنِسَةُ الْحَسْنَاءُ الَّتِي كَانَتْ تَتَحَدَّثُ مَعَكَ. إِنَّهُ لَسَعِيدُ الْحَظِّ مَنْ سَيَتَزَوَّجُهَا!" أَجَابَتْهُ الْمُرَبِّيَةُ فِي جَفَافٍ.

"مَاذَا؟ أَيَعْنِي هَذَا أَنَّهَا مِنْ عَائِلَةِ كَابُولِيت؟" قَالَ رُومِيُو فِي نَفْسِهِ. "أَيَعْنِي هَذَا أَنَّ حَيَاتِي أَصْبَحَتْ فِي أَيْدِي أَعْدَائِي؟" بَدَأَ رُومِيُو بِالتَّفْكِيرِ وَالتَّجْهِيمِ: مَاذَا سَيَكُونُ مَصِيرُهُ وَمَصِيرُ حُبِّهِ؟ كَيْفَ سَيُوَفِّقُ بَيْنَ حُبِّهِ وَكُرْهِهِ؟ بَيْنَ حَبِيبَتِهِ وَأَعْدَائِهِ؟...

غَادَرَ مَنْزِلَ كَابُولِيت وَفُؤَادُهُ مُحْتَرِقٌ بِالْأَسْئِلَةِ.

فِي مَنْزِلِ كَابُولِيت، أَمْسَكَتْ جُولِييت بِمُرَبِّيَتِهَا وَتَرَجَّتْهَا إِنْ كَانَتْ تَعْرِفُ حَبِيبَهَا: "قُولِي لِي أَرْجُوكِ مَنْ يَكُونُ؟ مَا اسْمُهُ؟ وَهَلْ هُوَ مُتَزَوِّجٌ؟ إِنْ كَانَ مُتَزَوِّجًا فَالْمَوْتُ أَرْفَقُ بِي مِنْ أَنْ أَتَزَوَّجَ غَيْرَهُ..."

"حَسَنًا، حَسَنًا، اِهْدَئي سَأُخْبِرُكِ! إِنَّهُ... إِنَّهُ روميو مُنتيغيو، الِابْنُ الْوَحيدُ لِعَدُوِّكِ اللَّدودِ يا آنِسَتي" رَدَّتِ المُرَبِّيَةُ.

"ماذا؟ أَهَذا يَعْني أَنَّ الرَّجُلَ الْوَحيدَ الَّذي وَقَعْتُ في حُبِّهِ يَكونُ ابْنَ الرَّجُلِ الْوَحيدِ الَّذي أَكْرَهُهُ؟ ما هذِهِ الصُّدْفَةُ الْغَريبَةُ؟ يا لَهُ مِن وَحْشٍ فَتَّاكٍ هذا الْحُبُّ الَّذي جَعَلَني أَقَعُ في فَخِّهِ وَأُغْرَمُ بِأَلَدِّ أَعْدائي! يا تُرى ماذا سَيَكونُ مَصيري وَمَصيرُ حُبِّي؟"

ظَلَّتِ الْمُرَبِّيَةُ صامِتَةً وَعَجَزَتْ عَنِ اسْتيعابِ مَدى خُطورَةِ وَقَسْوَةِ الْأَمْرِ.

# Vocabulary

### p. 24

نَظَّمَ (تَنْظيمٌ) [2s] to organize, arrange
جولييت Juliet *(name)*
تَجاذَبَ أَطْرافَ الْحَديثِ [6s] to chat
مُرَبِّيَةٌ nurse(maid), nanny
طُفولَةٌ childhood
غَرِقَ (غَرَقٌ) [1s4] to sink
تَمادَى في [6d] to be excessive in

مُزاحٌ jest, wit
نُكْتَةٌ (نِكاتٌ، نُكَتٌ) funny story, joke
سَخيفٌ (سُخَفاءُ) silly, ridiculous
سافِلٌ obscene, despicable
أَهَمِّيَّةٌ importance
جِدِّيَّةٌ seriousness, earnestness
اِسْتِعْدادٌ willingness, readiness

### p. 25

بَلَغَ (بُلوغٌ) [1s3] to attain, reach
أَشارَ إلَى [4h] to point out, indicate; to insinuate
أَفْصَحَ [4s] to clarify, express eloquently
اِخْتَصَرَ [8s1] to summarize, outline
شَهْمٌ (شُهومٌ) chivalrous
باسِلٌ (بَواسِلُ) valiant, brave
قاطَعَ [3s] to interrupt
مُتَحَمِّسٌ enthusiastic
عَدَّ (عَدٌّ) [1g3] to count, enumerate
أَحْصَى [4d] to count, enumerate

خَصْلَةٌ (خِصالٌ) quality, characteristic, trait
مِيزَةٌ (مَزايا) advantage
مِلْكٌ (أَمْلاكٌ) property, possession
لَفَتَ [1s2] to turn, direct
اِنْتِباهاً attention
خَتَمَ (خِتامٌ) [1s2] to end, bring to an end
مَدْحٌ (أَمْداحٌ) praise
أَعَدَّ سَهْرَةً [4g] to throw a party
أُعْجِبَ بِ [4s] *pass.* to admire, hold in high regard
بيتر Peter
جاهِزٌ ready

ضَيْفٌ (ضُيوفٌ) guest
مُتَشَوِّقٌ excited

رَأَى (رُؤْيَةٌ) [1d1(b)] to see

## p. 26

اِلْتَحَقَ بِ [8s1] to join
نَفَذَ (نَفاذٌ) [1s3] to convey, communicate
مَرْكوشْيو Mercutio (name)
مُتَنَكِّرٌ disguised, in disguise
قِناعٌ (أَقْنِعَةٌ) mask
تَفَطَّنَ لِ [5s] to discern, figure out
مَشْعَلٌ (مَشاعِلُ) torch, flame
مُتَوَتِّرٌ tense, nervous

طَمْأَنَ [11s(b)] to reassure
دَرَجٌ (أَدْراجٌ) way, route
رَغْبَةٌ desire
مُجْبَرٌ عَلَى forced to
مُغْرَمٌ in love
سَعِدَ (سَعادَةٌ) [1s4] to be happy
اِبْتَهَجَ [8s] to rejoice, be cheerful
اِسْتَحَقَّ [10g] to deserve
سَعادَةٌ happiness

## p. 27

عَنيفٌ (عُنُفٌ) tough, strenuous, violent
فَظٌّ rude, uncouth
قاسٍ harsh, brutal
حَسْرَةٌ heartbreak, sorrow
اِنْتَصَرَ عَلَى [8s1] to defeat, beat
حَتْمًا certainly, definitely
مُصَمِّمٌ determined
تَعاسَةٌ misfortune
تَشاؤُمٌ pessimism
حَدَثٌ (أَحْداثٌ) incident, happening, event

طارِئٌ (طَوارِئُ) unforeseen event
قَدَرٌ fate
لُعْبَةٌ (لَعَبٌ) game
تَبادَلَ أَطْرافَ الْحَديثِ [6s] to chat
تَسامَرَ [6s] to chat (in the evening)
أَلْقَى خِطابًا [4d] to give a speech
عَزيزٌ (أَعِزَّاءُ) dear
هَرِمَ (هَرَمٌ/مَهْرَمَةٌ) [1s4] to become decrepit
بَدَلَ instead of
موسيقِيٌّ musician

## p. 28

آلَةٌ instrument
أَمْتَعَ [4s] to entertain
حاضِرٌ attendee

دَرَى (دِرايَةٌ) [1d2] to know
فاقَ (فَوْقٌ) [1h3] to exceed, outdo
خَيالٌ (أَخْيِلَةٌ) imagination

| | |
|---|---|
| ضاهَى [3d] | to equal, match, rival |
| يَمامٌ coll. | doves |
| سِرْبٌ (أَسْرابٌ) | flock, swarm |
| غُرابٌ (غِرْبانٌ) | crow, raven |
| ذُهول | amazement |
| راقَبَ [3s] | to observe, watch |
| مَسْحورٌ | enchanted, fascinated |
| مُتَأَكِّدٌ | certain, sure |
| خَفَقَ (خَفَقانٌ) [1s3] | to pulsate, beat |
| حَقًّا | really |
| شَكٌّ (شُكوكٌ) | doubt |
| كاذِبٌ | lying, deceptive |
| حَقيقيٌّ | real, true |
| مُنْبَهِرٌ | overwhelmed, dazed, dazzled |

| | |
|---|---|
| اِسْتَشاطَ [10h] | to fume, boil over (with anger) |
| أَحْكَمَ [4s] | to tighten |
| قَبْضَةٌ | grip |
| هَمَّ بِ (هَمٌّ) [1g3] | to set off (to) |
| تَوَقَّفَ عَنْ [5s] | to stop, cease |
| عَيْبٌ (عُيوبٌ) | disadvantage, drawback, harm |
| حُضورٌ pl. | presence, attendance |
| أَرْجاءٌ pl. | area |
| شَهامَةٌ | chivalry, gallantry |
| أَخْلاقٌ pl. | ethics, morals |
| تَرَكَهُ وَشَأْنَهُ (تَرْكٌ) [1s3] | to leave (someone) alone |
| طَرْدٌ (طُرودٌ) | driving away, expulsion |

*p. 29*

| | |
|---|---|
| لَمْ يَزِدْ إِلّا | only, just, no more than |
| تَحْريضٌ | incitement, agitation |
| أُطْرِدَ [4s] pass. | to be kicked out, expelled (more correct: طُرِدَ) |
| مَرْأًى | view, sight |
| قاعَةٌ | hall |
| كَريمٌ (كِرامٌ) | noble, honorable |
| غَنَّى (غِناءٌ) [2d] | to sing |
| اِسْتَغَلَّ [10g] | to take advantage of |
| أَمْسَكَ [4s] | to hold |
| رِقَّةٌ | softness, delicacy |
| مَلْمَسٌ (مَلامِسُ) | touch, feel |
| مُعْجَبٌ بِ | impressed by |

| | |
|---|---|
| وَسيمٌ (وِسامٌ) | handsome |
| فَكَّرَ بِ [2s] | to think about |
| وَسامَةٌ | handsomeness, good looks |
| غافَلَ [3s] | to surprise, take by surprise |
| تَقْبيلٌ (تَقابيلُ) | kissing |
| فَزِعَ (فَزَعٌ) [1s1] | to panic; be afraid |
| اِمْتَنَعَ [8s1] | to decline, refuse |
| خَجَلٌ | shyness, coyness |
| غازَلَ [3s] | to flirt with |
| مَفْتونٌ بِ | infatuated with |
| حُسْنٌ (مَحاسِنُ) | beauty, prettiness |

| | |
|---|---|
| اِخْتَطَفَ [8s1] to abduct, kidnap | أُعْجِبَ [8s1] pass. to be impressed |
| (قُبَلٌ) قُبْلَةٌ kiss | قَبَّلَ [2s] to kiss |
| (شَفايِفُ) شَفَةٌ lip | فارَقَ [3s] to detach, separate from |
| وَجْنَةٌ cheek | نَظْرَةٌ look, view, sight |

*p. 30*

| | |
|---|---|
| إِعْجابٌ admiration | (مَصائِرُ) مَصيرٌ fate, destiny |
| تَساءَلَ [6s(b)] to inquire, ask | وَفَّقَ بَيْنَ [2s] to reconcile, bring into agreement |
| فاضِلٌ virtuous | غادَرَ [3s] to leave, depart |
| تَرْبِيَةٌ education, upbringing | (أَفْئِدَةٌ) فُؤادٌ heart |
| آنِسَةٌ young lady, miss | مُحْتَرِقٌ burning, ablaze |
| حَظٌّ luck | تَرَجَّى [5d] to beg |
| جَفافٌ dryness | مُتَزَوِّجٌ married |
| تَخْمينٌ guess, conjecture | |

*p. 31*

| | |
|---|---|
| أَخْبَرَ [4s] to tell | يا تُرى I wonder... |
| وَحيدٌ sole, only, lone | (ضَلالٌ) ظَلَّ [1g2] to remain, continue (to be) |
| (أَعْداءٌ) عَدُوٌّ enemy | صامِتٌ silent |
| (صُدَفٌ) صُدْفَةٌ coincidence | (عَجْزٌ) عَجَزَ عَنْ [1s2] to be unable to |
| فَتّاكٌ lethal, deadly | اِسْتيعابٌ comprehension |
| (وُقوعٌ) وَقَعَ [1a1] to fall | قَسْوَةٌ severity, hardness |
| (فُخوخٌ) فَخٌّ snare, trap | |
| أُغْرِمَ بِ [4s] pass. to be in love with | |
| أَلَدُّ عَدُوٍّ archenemy | |

## Translation

*p. 24*

While the servants were busy preparing for the party, organizing the tables at the Capulets' residence, Lady Capulet was, together with her daughter Juliet and the nanny, in one of the rooms, chatting.

The nanny began to reminisce about the days of Juliet's childhood and became absorbed in talking about those days going to extremes in telling silly and obscene jokes which angered Juliet and her mother. Lady Capulet quickly changed the subject to address a more important and serious issue: Juliet's age and her willingness to marry.

*p. 25*

Lady Capulet was trying hard to convince her daughter, who was not yet 14 years old, of the idea of getting married early, noting that many of the girls of Verona had gotten married at a young age and were happy in their marriages.

She quickly told her, "I will cut to the point, my daughter; Lord Paris, that young and valiant gentleman, wants you to be his wife."

"What a man! He is such a great man!" the nanny interrupted her excitedly.

Lady Capulet continued to enumerate Paris' qualities and characteristics, especially his real estate, in an attempt to get Juliet's attention, and concluded her praise by telling her daughter that he was coming to the party that her father was throwing.

Juliet began to be persuaded by the words of her mother and her nanny and promised to try to appreciate him during the party.

As they chatted, Peter, the Capulet's servant, entered and interrupted them. "Madam, dinner is ready and the guests have come and are waiting for you. They are excited to see…

*p. 26*

Miss Juliet. Come and join them before they get impatient."

"Come on, Juliet, hurry up!" Lady Capulet shouted.

൞ ൞ ൞

In the meantime, Romeo, his cousin Benvolio, and their friend Mercutio entered the Capulet's palace disguised to keep out of sight. They were accompanied by five or six masked men carrying torches. Romeo looked a little nervous, but Benvolio reassured him that they would dance a little and enjoy the evening and then go back home.

"No, Benvolio," Romeo replied sadly. "I feel sad… I have no desire to dance. Give me that torch and go dance."

"No, my dear friend," replied Mercutio. "You have to dance and you will dance. You are in love and so you have to be happy and cheerful and dance. Love is a beautiful and delicate feeling worthy of happiness!"

*p. 27*

"Really? I'd rather say it's rough, rude, and rowdy," Romeo answered him with sorrow.

"Well, well, if love is so, you have to be tough with it too, and you will certainly defeat it!"

As usual, Romeo was not convinced by Mercutio's words, while the latter was determined to help Romeo emerge from his grief and misfortune.

As for Romeo, he concluded his pessimism saying, "Anyway, I feel that tonight's party will be the beginning of something bad that may befall me... of an event or an incident that will end with my death... but... don't worry... may fate play its game! Come on, boys! Let's go in!"

ஒ ஒ ஒ

The guests had gathered at the Capulets' Palace. They were chatting and conversing, drinking, and eating. Lord Capulet stood by and gave a short speech to the invited guests. "Welcome my dear guests. Enjoy the party, and dance, for I am too old to dance like you... so, dance instead of me. And you musicians! Play...

*p. 28*

your instruments and let us enjoy your music. Welcome, everyone! Have a good evening!"

Everyone began to dance, but Romeo stayed away, staring at the guests. Perhaps he was looking for his sweetheart, Rosaline. Who knows?

Suddenly, he spotted a girl more beautiful than he could even imagine. Her tenderness rivalled the tenderness of doves. She seemed to him like a dove amid a flock of crows. He stood in amazement watching her and her movements as if he were enchanted and asked himself, "Am I sure that my heart has ever really beaten before this time? No! I do not think so. There's no doubt that my eyes were liars; this is the first time I've ever seen real beauty!"

While Romeo was being dazzled by the beauty of the girl, Tybalt, her cousin, became aware of his presence. He was furious and quickly tightened his grip on his weapon and hurried in the direction of Romeo yelling and swearing. Everyone stopped dancing.

Tybalt's uncle, Lord Capulet, intervened and tried to calm him down. "Please calm down, son. What is the harm in his presence? Also, he is known throughout Verona for his grace and noble morals. Leave him alone! Please... I cannot drive him out of my house!"

*p. 29*

However, this only increased the agitation and stubbornness in Tybalt, which angered Lord Capulet, and so he kicked Tybalt out of the party in front of everyone. Tybalt obeyed his uncle's orders and went out of the hall, threatening Romeo while everyone looked at him.

"Carry on dancing! Enjoy your party, my honored guests!" Lord Capulet cheered to the attendees. Everyone went back to dancing and singing.

Romeo used the opportunity to approach the beautiful girl, who had robbed his mind and held her hand dazzled by the softness of her touch. She also seemed to be impressed by him. He was really a very handsome young man! She unleashed her imagination fancying about him and his handsomeness.

Suddenly, Romeo took her by surprise, trying to kiss her, but she panicked and shyly refused. He continued flirting with her, fascinated by her beauty and her tenderness. He stole a quick kiss from her lips. Juliet blushed, but she fell in love with Romeo and was impressed with his kiss and kissed him in return, and her heart was beating, and her eyes did not leave his eyes...

It was love at first sight!

*p. 30*

They exchanged looks of love and admiration in

silence until the nanny interrupted them. "Miss! Your mother wants you right away!"

"Who might her mother be?" inquired Romeo.

"Her mother is the lady of this house! A great and virtuous lady. I was the one who raised her daughter... Juliet, that beautiful young woman who was talking to you. Lucky is the one who will marry her!" The nanny answered him firmly.

"What? Does that mean she is a Capulet?" Romeo wondered. "Does this mean that my life is in the hands of my enemies?" Romeo began to think and conjecture. What would be his fate and the fate of his love? How will he reconcile between his love and his hatred? And between his beloved and his enemies?

He left the Capulets' house, his heart burning with questions.

ഈ ഈ ഈ

At the Capulets', Juliet held onto her nanny and begged her if she knew her love. "Tell me, please, what is his name, and is he married? If he is married, death would be better for me than marrying someone else."

*p. 31*

"All right, calm down and I'll tell you! He is... he is... Romeo Montague, the only son of your archenemy, my lady," the nanny replied.

"What? Does this mean that the only man I've fallen in love with is the son of the only man I hate? What is this strange coincidence? What a deadly monster this love is! This love that entrapped me into its net and made me fall in love with my worst enemies! I wonder, what will be my destiny and the fate of my love?"

The nanny remained silent, unable to comprehend the gravity and severity of the matter.

# اَلْفَصْلُ الثَّالِثُ

في لَحَظاتٍ مَعْدودَةٍ اِنْطَفَأَ حُبُّ رومْيو لِروزالايْن لِيَأْخُذَ مَكانَهُ حُبُّ جوليِيتْ الَّتي سَلَبَتْهُ عَقْلَهُ وَفِكْرَهُ، وَوَجَدَ نَفْسَهُ غَيْرَ قادِرٍ عَلَى التَّفْكيرِ إِلَّا بِها...

جوليِيتْ، تِلْكَ الْفَتاةُ الْجَميلَةُ الَّتي مِنَ الْمُفْتَرَضِ أَنْ تَكونَ عَدُوَّتَهُ اللَّدودَةَ هِا هُوَ يَقَعُ في شِباكِ غَرامِها. فَمَتى وَكَيْفَ سَيُعَبِّرُ لَها عَنْ مَدى شَوْقِهِ وَلَوْعَتِهِ؟ وَماذا عَنْ مَشاعِرِها هِيَ يا تُرى؟ هَلْ تُبادِلُهُ الْإِحْساسَ؟ هَلْ تُحِبُّهُ؟ وَإِنْ كانَتْ تُحِبُّهُ، فَكَيْفَ وَأَيْنَ سَيَلْتَقِيانِ بَعيدًا عَنْ أَعْيُنِ النَّاسِ؟ كُلُّ هَذِهِ الْأَسْئِلَةِ كانَتْ تَجوبُ في خاطِرِ رومْيو

الْعاشِقُ الْوَلْهانُ، وَلَعَلَّها كانَتْ تَدورُ أَيْضًا في ذِهْنِ جوليِيت... مَنْ يَدْري؟

إِلَّا أَنَّ الْحُبَّ أَرْسَلَ لَهُما شُحْنَةً مِنَ الْقُوَّةِ وَالصُّمودِ، وَبِتَوافُقٍ مَعَ الزَّمَنِ وَرُبَّما مَعَ الْقَدَرِ، مُنِحَ الْعاشِقانِ فُرْصَةَ اللِّقاءِ مُجَدَّدًا، وَيا لَها مِنْ فُرْصَةٍ سَخِيَّةٍ مَحَتْ كُلَّ الْعَراقيلِ وَالْمَخاطِرِ، الَّتي واجَهَها الشَّابّانِ الْعاشِقانِ، وَإِنْ كانَ ذَلِكَ لِفَتْرَةٍ زَمَنِيَّةٍ وَجيزَةٍ فَقَطْ.

فَعِنْدَ خُروجِهِمْ مِنْ قَصْرِ كابوليت، اِبْتَعَدَ روميو عَنْ بَنْفوليو وَمَرْكوشيو وَاخْتَفى عَنْ مَرْآهُما وَاجْتَمى بِالظَّلامِ. حاوَلا جاهِدَيْنِ التَّفْتيشَ عَنْهُ وَلَكِنْ دونَ جَدْوى. فَنَظَرَ مَرْكوشيو إِلى بَنْفوليو وَقالَ لَهُ مُسْتَغْرِبًا: "هَيّا يا بَنْفوليو لِنَذْهَبَ مِنْ هُنا... لَقَدِ اخْتَفى."

"مَعَكَ حَقٌّ مَرْكوشيو. ما الْفائِدَةُ في الْبَحْثِ عَنْهُ إِنْ كانَ لا يُريدُنا أَنْ نَجِدَهُ؟ لِنَذْهَبْ" أَجابَهُ بَنْفوليو.

فَعادا إِلى مَنازِلِهِما مُتْعَبَيْنِ مِنَ السَّهْرَةِ.

في هَذِهِ الْأَثْناءِ، تَسَلَّلَ روميو إِلى مَنْزِلِ كابوليت وَاحْتَمى بِالشُّجَيْراتِ

تَحْتَ شُرْفَةِ جولييت دونَ أَنْ تَلْحَظَ هَذِهِ الأَخيرةُ وُجودَهُ.

لَمَحَ حَبيبَتَهُ فَقالَ مُخاطِبًا نَفْسَهُ: "ما هَذا النُّورُ الَّذي يُطِلُّ مِنْ شُرْفَتِها؟ أَهِيَ حَبيبَتي؟ نَعَمْ إِنَّها هِيَ... آهٍ لَوْ كانَتْ تَعْلَمُ كَمْ أُحِبُّها... وَكَمْ أُفَكِّرُ بها... وَكَمْ أَنا مُشْتاقٌ لِمَلْقاها! ما أَجْمَلَها! وَما أَرَقَّها! آهٍ! كَمْ أُحِبُّها! لَيْتَني أَسْتَطيعُ لَمْسَ وَجْنَتَيْها الْمُشِعَّتَيْنِ نورًا! أَرْجوكِ تَكَلَّمي، تَكَلَّمي، أَيُّها الْمَلاكُ الْمُضيءُ!"

في هَذا الْوَقْتِ كانَتْ جولييت في غُرْفَتِها. كانَ قَلْبُها يَخْفِقُ حُبًّا وَاشْتِياقًا لِروميو. وَقَفَتْ في شُرْفَتِها مُحَدِّثَةً نَفْسَها دونَ أَنْ تَعْلَمَ بِوُجودِهِ: "روميو حَبيبي! لِمَ كُتِبَ عَلَيْكَ أَنْ تَحْمِلَ هَذا الاسْمَ؟ لِمَ لا تَتَجَرَّدُ مِنَ اسْمِكَ وَمِنْ عائِلَتِكَ؟ لِمَ لا تُغَيِّرُ اسْمَكَ؟ لِمَ؟ أَوْ... إِنْ كُنْتَ لا تَرْغَبُ في تَغْييرِ اسْمِكَ، فَيَكْفيني أَنْ تَقولَ لي أَنَّكَ تُحِبُّني لِكَيْ أَنْسى أَنَّني كُنْتُ في يَوْمٍ مِنَ الأَيَّامِ مِنْ عائِلَةِ كابوليت. أَنْتَ لَسْتَ عَدُوِّي... اسْمُكَ هُوَ عَدُوِّي! إِذَنْ أَنْتَ لَنْ تَتَغَيَّرَ إِنْ غَيَّرْتَ اسْمَكَ! فَما الَّذي يَمْنَعُكَ مِنْ ذَلِكَ؟ أَنْتَ قادِرٌ عَلى تَغْييرِهِ. أَرْجوكَ غَيِّرْهُ! فَما هِيَ أَهَمِّيَّةُ الأَسْماءِ؟ فَهِيَ أَبَدًا لا تَدُلُّ عَلى مُسَمَّياتِها. فَالْوَرْدَةُ سَتَظَلُّ رائِحَتُها طَيِّبَةً وَإِنْ سَمَّيْناها بِأَسْماءٍ أُخْرى. أَرْجوكَ حَبيبي روميو، انْزِعْ عَنْكَ هَذا الاسْمَ، وَخُذْني أَنا بَديلَةً."

كانَ رومْيو يَسْتَمِعُ إِلَى كُلِّ كَلِمَةٍ تَفَوَّهَتْ بِها جولِييت. فَاسْتَجْمَعَ قِواهُ وَاقْتَرَبَ بِبُطْءٍ مِنْ شُرْفَتِها وَتَكَلَّمَ مُخاطِبًا إِيَّاها: "أَثِقُ بِكِ يا حَبيبَتي وَأَثِقُ بِكُلِّ كَلِمَةٍ قُلْتِها، فَقَطْ أَطْلُبُ مِنْكِ أَنْ تُخْبِريني إِنْ كُنْتِ تُحِبّينَني وَسَأَسْتَعيرُ اسْمًا آخَرَ بَدَلَ اسْمي، وَلَنْ أَكونَ رومْيو مُنْتيغْيو مُجَدَّدًا!"

إِنْتَفَضَتْ جولِييت فَزَعًا وَقالَتْ في اِضْطِرابٍ: "مَنْ هُنا؟ مَنْ أَنْتَ؟ وَماذا تَفْعَلُ هُنا في شُرْفَتي؟ وَكَيْفَ تَسَلَّلْتَ إِلَى هُنا؟ وَلِمَ أَنْتَ مُخْتَبِئٌ في الظَّلامِ تَسْتَرِقُ السَّمْعَ إِلَى خَواطِري؟"

"لا أَعْرِفُ كَيْفَ سَأُعَرِّفُ بِنَفْسي فَأَنا أَكْرَهُ اسْمي، فَإِنَّ اسْمي يَكونُ عَدُوَّكِ!" أَجابَها رومْيو.

"رومْيو؟ رومْيو مُنْتيغْيو؟" سَأَلَتْهُ جولِييت في تَعَجُّبٍ وَذُهولٍ.

"لا، لَسْتُ بِرومْيو... وَلا بِمُنْتيغْيو إِنْ كُنْتِ تَكْرَهينَهُما..."

تَذَكَّرَتْ جولِييت اَلْكَلامَ الَّذي قالَتْهُ مُنْذُ حينٍ مُخاطِبَةً نَفْسَها، فاحْمَرَّتْ وَجْنَتاها خَجَلًا وَسَأَلَتْهُ: "كَيْفَ تَمَكَّنْتَ مِنَ الصُّعودِ إِلَى شُرْفَتي؟ فَالتَّسَلُّقُ مِنْ عَلَى السُّورِ صَعْبٌ لِلْغايَةِ، كَيْفَ فَعَلْتَ ذَلِكَ؟"

فَأجابَها روميو في فَخْرٍ: "إنَّ حُبَّكِ قَدْ مَنَحَني أَجْنِحَةً لِأَطيرَ بِها حَيْثُما شِئْتُ..."

اِقْتَرَبَ مِنْ شُرْفَتِها أَكْثَرَ، وظَلَّا يَتَحَدَّثانِ عَنْ حُبِّهِما وَيبوحانِ بِأَسْرارِهِما لِبَعْضِهِما الْبَعْض، فَهُما عَلَى يَقينٍ مِنْ أَنَّ هَذا الْحُبَّ قَدْ يُشَكِّلُ خَطَرًا عَلَيْهِما وَمِنْ أَنَّ هَذِهِ الْعَلاقَةَ قَدْ تَنْتَهي بِمَقْتَلِ روميو إِنْ تَفَطَّنَ أَحَدُهُمْ إِلَى وُجودِهِ، إِلَّا أَنَّ روميو كانَ مُسْتَعِدًّا لِمُواجَهَةِ الْمَوْتِ في سَبيلِ جولييت. فَحاوَلَ إِقْناعَها بِبَساطَةِ الْأَمْرِ وَطَمْأَنَها مُقْسِمًا لَها بِحُبِّهِ وَوَلائِهِ لَها، فَهَدَّأَ قَليلًا مِنْ خَوْفِها وَتَرَدُّدِها.

قَبْلَ أَنْ تُوَدِّعَهُ، تَرَجَّتْهُ أَنْ يَفِيَ بِوَعْدِهِ وَأَنْ يَظَلَّ مُخْلِصًا لَها وَأَنْ يُفَكِّرَ بِها إِلَى أَنْ يَلْتَقِيا مُجَدَّدًا.

فَأَعْرَبَ لَها روميو عَنْ حُزْنِهِ الشَّديدِ لِفِراقِها قائِلًا: "يا لَهُ مِنْ لِقاءٍ جَميلٍ حَبيبَتي! خَوْفي أَنْ يَكونَ كُلُّ هَذا حُلُمٌ سَأَسْتَيْقِظُ مِنْهُ لِأُواجِهَ واقِعًا مَريرًا! فَإِنَّ هَذا اللِّقاءَ رائِعٌ جِدًّا لِيَكونَ حَقيقيًّا..." وَفَجْأَةً، سَمِعَتْ جولييت مُرَبِّيَتَها تُناديها مِنَ الدَّاخِلِ فَأَجابَتْهُ مُسْرِعَةً: "حَبيبي روميو، إِنْ كُنْتَ فِعْلًا تُحِبُّني وإِنْ كانَتْ نَواياكَ فِعْلًا حَسَنَةً وَتُريدُني زَوْجَةً لَكَ سَوْفَ أُرْسِلُ لَكَ غَدًا رَسولًا سَتُخْبِرُني عَنْ طَريقِهِ مَتَى وَأَيْنَ

سَنَتَزَوَّج، وَأَنَا أَعِدُكَ أَنْ أَتْرُكَ كُلَّ شَيْءٍ وَرَائِي وَأَرْحَلَ مَعَكَ..."

"آنِسَتِي!" هَتَفَتِ المُرَبِّيَّةُ تُنَادِي جوليِيت مَرَّةً أُخْرى.

"آتِيَةٌ! آتِيَةٌ!" أَجَابَتْها جوليِيت.

"مَتَى أُرْسِلُهُ إِلَيْكَ؟" سَأَلَتْ جوليِيت حَبِيبَها.

"عَلَى السَّاعَةِ التَّاسِعَةِ،" رَدَّ روميو.

وَدَّعَ بَعْضُهُما البَعْضَ في أَسَى عَلَى أَمَلِ لِقَاءٍ قَرِيبٍ، وَهَرَعَتْ جوليِيت إِلَى الدَّاخِلِ، وَقَدْ بَدَا لَها المَنْزِلُ وَكَأَنَّهُ سِجْنٌ كُتِبَ عَلَيْها أَنْ تَسْكُنَهُ وَأَنْ تَرْضَخَ لِقَوانِينِ سَاكِنِيهِ. أَمَّا روميو، فَعَادَ أَدْرَاجَهُ وَقَدْ مَلَأَ الحُزْنُ قَلْبَهُ مِنْ جَدِيدٍ.

---

كَانَ الوَقْتُ فَجْرًا وَبَدَأَتِ السَّاعَاتُ تَطُولُ وَتَطُولُ وَكَأَنَّها سِنِينٌ تَمُرُّ مِنْ عُمْرِهِ. فَفِرَاقُها كَانَ أَقْسَى بِكَثِيرٍ مِمَّا كَانَ يَتَخَيَّلُ.

تَذَكَّرَ روميو القِسِّيسَ لورِنْس، فَقَصَدَهُ مَهْرُولًا لَعَلَّهُ يُزَوِّجُهُما سِرًّا.

كَانَ القِسِّيسُ لورنس يَحْمِلُ سَلَّةً وَمُنْهَمِكًا في جَمْعِ الأَعْشَابِ

وَالزُّهُورِ. كَانَ يَتَغَنَّى بِالطَّبِيعَةِ وَبِجَمَالِهَا وَعَطَائِهَا، مُمْسِكًا بِزَهْرَةٍ فِي يَدِهِ. قَالَ مُخَاطِبًا نَفْسَهُ: "وَسَطَ هَذِهِ الزَّهْرَةِ الضَّئِيلَةِ يَكْمُنُ سُمٌّ قَاتِلٌ، وَفِي الآنِ ذَاتِهِ، يَكْمُنُ عِلَاجٌ فَعَّالٌ. فَإِنِ اسْتَنْشَقْتَهَا، سَيَسْرِي فِي كَامِلِ جَسَدِكَ إِحْسَاسٌ رَائِعٌ يُشْفِيكَ مِنْ كُلِّ عِلَّةٍ، أَمَّا إِذَا تَذَوَّقْتَهَا، فَسَتَتَسَمَّمُ حَتْمًا وَتَمُوتُ! كُلُّ شَيْءٍ فِي هَذَا الْكَوْنِ يَحْمِلُ فِي طَيَّاتِهِ عُنْصُرَيْنِ مُتَضَادَّيْنِ، تَمَامًا مِثْلَ الْإِنْسَانِ؛ فَهُوَ يَحْمِلُ فِي ذَاتِهِ الْخَيْرَ وَالشَّرَّ مَعًا..." قَطَعَ رُومِيُو جَمْلَ أَفْكَارِ الْقِسِّيسِ مُلْقِيًا عَلَيْهِ التَّحِيَّةَ، فَأَجَابَهُ لُورِنْسُ مُتَعَجِّبًا: "رُومِيُو! مَاذَا تَفْعَلُ هُنَا؟ وَلِمَ أَنْتَ صَاحٍ فِي هَذَا الْوَقْتِ الْبَاكِرِ؟ أَلَمْ تَنَمْ؟ هَلْ كُنْتَ مَعَ روزالاين؟"

"روزالاين؟ لَا! لَقَدْ نَسِيتُهَا يَا أَبَتِ!"

"إِذًا أَيْنَ كُنْتَ؟" سَأَلَهُ لُورِنْسُ.

"كُنْتُ فِي مَنْزِلِ أَعْدَائِي... اجْتَفَلْتُ مَعَهُمْ، فَوَقَعْتُ فِي شِبَاكِ الْحُبِّ أَوْ عَلَى الْأَحْرَى... وَقَعْتُ فِي فَخِّهِ، وَأُصِبْتُ بِجُرُوحٍ بَلِيغَةٍ... وَعَمِيقَةٍ يَا أَبَتِ... وَلَا أَحَدَ يَقْدِرُ عَلَى مُعَالَجَتِهَا سِوَاكَ!"

بَدَا لُورِنْسُ حَائِرًا فِي أَمْرِ رُومِيُو وَطَلَبَ مِنْهُ أَنْ يُوَضِّحَ لَهُ مَا يَقْصِدُ، فَأَجَابَهُ: "أَنَا أُحِبُّ جُولِييت، ابْنَةَ السَّيِّدِ كَابُولِيتْ... وَهِيَ كَذَلِكَ

تُحِبُّني... سَأُخْبِرُكَ في وَقْتٍ لاحِقٍ عَنْ مَتى وَأَيْنَ وَكَيْفَ التَقَيْنا، وَلَكِنَّ الْمُهِمَّ الآنَ أَنْ تُزَوِّجَنا وَتُبارِكَ زَواجَنا..." كادَ الْقِسِّيسُ لورِنْسْ يَفْقِدُ صَوابَهُ مِنْ هَذا الْخَبَرِ، فَهُوَ قَدْ عَهِدَ روميو يَبْكي كُلَّ يَوْمٍ عَلَى روزالايْنْ... فَرَدَّ عَلَيْهِ مُتَفاجِئًا: "ماذا؟ أَبِهَذِهِ السُّرْعَةِ نَسيتَها وَنَسيتَ حُبَّها؟ كَمْ مِنْ دَمْعَةٍ ذَرَفْتِها مِنْ أَجْلِها؟ وَكَمْ مِنْ لَيْلَةٍ سَهِرْتَ تَبْكيها؟ ما الَّذي حَدَثَ لَكَ يا ابْني؟ أَبِهَذِهِ السُّرْعَةِ أَحْبَبْتَ غَيْرَها؟ مَعَكَ حَقٌّ... فَالشَّبابُ يُحِبُّونَ بِعُيونِهِمْ وَلَيْسَ بِقُلوبِهِمْ فَلِذَلِكَ لا تَتَوَقَّعوا أَنْ تَكونَ الْفَتَياتُ مُخْلِصاتٍ لَكُمْ في ظِلِّ خِياناتِكُمْ هَذِهِ!"

"أَلَسْتَ أَنْتَ الَّذي نَهَرْتَني عَنْ روزالايْنْ وَجَذَّرْتَني مِنْ حُبِّها؟ أَلَسْتَ أَنْتَ الَّذي شَجَّعْتَني عَلَى نِسْيانِها وَدَفْنِ حُبِّها يا أَبَتِ؟" سَأَلَهُ روميو في عِتابٍ وَحُزْنٍ.

"يا ابْني! أَنا لَمْ أَطْلُبْ مِنْكَ دَفْنَ حُبٍّ لِأَجِدَكَ مَهْووسًا بِحُبٍّ آخَرَ... أَقْسَى وَأَخْطَرَ مِنَ الْأَوَّلِ!"

"أَرْجوكَ يا أَبَتِ ساعِدْني! أَتَوَسَّلُ إِلَيْكَ أَنْ تُساعِدَنا! زَوِّجْنا أَرْجوكَ! فَأَنا حَقًّا أُحِبُّها وَهِيَ تُحِبُّني!"

لَمْ يَكُنِ الْقِسِّيسُ لورِنْسْ مُقْتَنِعًا أَبَدًا بِتَسَرُّعِ روميو، إِلَّا أَنَّهُ أَشْفَقَ عَلَيْهِ،

فَوَعَدَهُ أَنْ يُزَوِّجَهُما سِرًّا.

## Vocabulary

### p. 42

مَعْدودٌ numbered, very few
إِنْطَفَأَ [7s(a)] to burn out
(أَخْذٌ) أَخَذَ [1s3(a)] to take
مُفْتَرَضْ supposed
ها (emphatic particle)
(وُقوعٌ) وَقَعَ في شِباكِ غَرامِهِ [1a1] to fall in love with (someone)
(أَشْواقٌ) شَوْقٌ longing, yearning

لَوْعَةٌ anguish
مَشاعِرُ pl. feelings
بادَلَ [3s] to requite, reciprocate
اِلْتَقى بِـ [8d1] to meet
(جَوْبٌ) جابَ في [1h3] to pierce, penetrate
(خَواطِرُ) خاطِرٌ mind; thought

### p. 43

(عُشّاقٌ) عاشِقٌ in love; lover
وَلْهانُ confused, bewildered
(أَذْهانٌ) ذِهْنٌ mind
أَرْسَلَ [4s] to send
شُحْنَةٌ load, shipment
(قِوى) قُوَّةٌ strength, energy, power
صُمودٌ resistance, steadfastness
تَوافُقٌ agreement, harmony
(مَنْحٌ) مُنِحَ [1s1] pass. to be granted, given
مُجَدَّدًا again
يا لَها مِن f. what a...!

(أَسْخِياءُ) سَخِيٌّ generous, liberal, abundant
(مَحْوٌ) مَحا [1d3] to erase, delete
(عَراقيلُ) عَرْقَلَةٌ obstacle
مَخاطِرُ pl. risks, dangers perils
(مُواجَهَةٌ) واجَهَ [3s] to face, confront
(شَبابٌ) شابٌّ young person, youth
فَتْرَةٌ زَمَنِيَّةٌ period of time
وَجيزٌ brief, short
اِحْتَمى [8d1] to hide
ظَلامٌ darkness
تَفْتيشٌ عَنْ search for
جَدْوى benefit, gain

مُسْتَغْرِبٌ surprising
لِنَذْهَبْ let's go
فَائِدَةٌ (فَوَائِدُ) benefit, use

تَسَلَّلَ إِلَى [5s] to infiltrate
شُجَيْرَةٌ shrub, bush

## p. 44

شُرْفَةٌ balcony
لَحَظَ (لَحْظٌ/لَحَظَانٌ) [1s1] to notice
أَطَلَّ [4g] to appear, come into view
مُشْتَاقٌ missing
مَلْقًى meeting, rendezvous
رَقِيقٌ delicate; *elative* أَرَقُّ
لَيْتَنِي I wish I...
لَمْسٌ touch(ing)
مُشِعٌّ glowing
مَلَاكٌ (مَلَائِكَةٌ) angel
مُضِيءٌ luminous, bright
اِشْتِيَاقٌ missing
لِمَ why

حَمَلَ (حَمْلٌ) [1s2] to bear, carry
تَجَرَّدَ مِنْ [5s] to get rid of
إِذَنْ so, therefore
دَلَّ عَلَى (دَلَالَةٌ) [1g3] to signify, denote
مُسَمًّى (مُسَمَّيَات) designation, name
رَائِحَةٌ (رَوَائِحُ) smell, scent, aroma
نَزَعَ عَنْ (نَزْعٌ) [1s1] to remove, discard
بَدِيلَةٌ (بَدَائِلُ) alternative, substitute

## p. 45

تَفَوَّهَ بِ [5s] to utter
اِسْتَجْمَعَ [10s] to gather
بِبُطْءٍ slowly
إِيَّا + pronoun suffix *(acts as object pronoun)*
وَثِقَ بِ (ثِقَةٌ) [1a2] to trust
اِسْتَعَارَ [10h] to borrow
اِنْتَفَضَ [8s1] to flounce, shake
فَزَعٌ (أَفْزَاعٌ) fright, horror, panic
اِضْطِرَابٌ befuddlement, confusion

مُخْتَبِئٌ hiding
اِسْتَرَقَ [10s] to eavesdrop
عَرَّفَ بِ [2s] to make known
تَعَجُّبٌ wonder, astonishment
اِحْمَرَّ [9s] to turn red
تَمَكَّنَ مِنْ [5s] to manage, be able to
صُعُودٌ ascent
تَسَلُّقٌ climbing over, scaling
سُورٌ (أَسْوَارٌ) wall
لِلْغَايَةِ extremely

## p. 46

فَخْرٌ pride
مَنَحَ (مَنْحٌ) [1s1] to allow, grant to
جَناحٌ (أَجْنِحَةٌ) wings
طارَ (طَيَرانٌ) [1h2] to fly
حَيْثُما wherever, anywhere
شاءَ (مَشيئَةٌ) [1h1(a)] to want
عَلَى يَقينٍ مِنْ certain of
شَكَّلَ [2s] to form
خَطَرٌ (أَخْطارٌ) danger
اِنْتَهَى [8d1] to end, be over
مَقْتَلٌ (مَقاتِلُ) killing, death, murder
في سَبيلِ for
أَقْسَمَ [4s] swearing; مُقْسِمٌ to swear, vow
وَلاءٌ loyalty
تَرَدُّدٌ hesitation

تَوَدَّعَ [5s] to bid farewell to
وَفَى بِ (وَفاءٌ) [1d2(b)] to carry out, fulfill (imperfect: يَفي)
وَعْدٌ (وُعودٌ) promise
مُخْلِصٌ faithful, honest, loyal
فِراقٌ leaving, parting; separation
اِسْتَيْقَظَ [10s] to wake up
مَريرٌ bitter
رائِعٌ (رَوائِعُ) wonderful, excellent
نادَى [3d] to call
مُسْرِعٌ quick, in a hurry
نِيَّةٌ (نَوايا) intention
حَسَنٌ (حِسانٌ) good
رَسولٌ (رُسُلٌ) messenger
طَريقٌ (طُرُقٌ) road

## p. 47

وَراءَ behind
رَحَلَ (رَحيلٌ) [1s1] to go away
تاسِعٌ (تَواسِعٌ) ninth
أَسًى sorrow, sadness
أَمَلٌ (آمالٌ) hope
سِجْنٌ (سُجونٌ) prison
سَكَنَ (سُكونٌ) [1s3] to inhabit; live (in)
رَضَخَ لِ (رُضوخٌ) [1s1] to submit, conform to
ساكِنٌ inhabitant, resident

مَلَأَ (مَلْءٌ) [1s1(b)] to fill
طالَ (طولٌ) [1h3] to go on, continue, stretch
مَرَّ (مَرٌّ/مُرورٌ) [1g3] to pass
أَقْسَى more difficult
قِسّيسٌ priest
لورِنْسْ Lawrence (name)
مُهَرْوِلٌ in a hurry, hasteful
زَوَّجَ [2s] to marry
سَلَّةٌ basket

| | |
|---|---|
| مُنْهَمِكٌ في engrossed, absorbed in | أَعْشابٌ pl. herbs |

*p. 48*

| | |
|---|---|
| عَطاءٌ endowment | عُنْصُرٌ (عَناصِرُ) element, component |
| ضَئيلٌ tiny, puny | مُتَضادٌّ opposite |
| كَمَنَ (كُمونٌ) [1s3] to be hidden, concealed | شَرٌّ (شُرورٌ) evil |
| سُمٌّ (سُمومٌ) poison | حَبْلُ أَفْكارٍ train of thought |
| قاتِلٌ (قَتَلَةٌ) lethal; murderous; murderer | تَحِيَّةٌ greeting |
| | مُتَعَجِّبٌ amazed, astonished |
| في الآنِ ذاتِهِ at the same time | يا أَبَتِ O Father! |
| عِلاجٌ remedy, treatment | إذًا so, then |
| فَعّالٌ effective | اِحْتَفَلَ [8s1] to celebrate |
| اِسْتَنْشَقَ [10s] to inhale | عَلَى أَحْرَى rather; more accurately |
| سَرَى (سَرَيانٌ) [1d2] to flow | أُصيبَ [4h] *pass.* to be wounded |
| جَسَدٌ (أَجْسادٌ) body | جُرْحٌ (جُروحٌ) wound, injury |
| أَشْفَى [4d] to heal | بَليغٌ (بُلَغاءُ) intense |
| عِلَّةٌ (عِلَلٌ) ailment, sickness | عَميقٌ (عِماقٌ) deep |
| تَذَوَّقَ [5s] to taste | مُعالَجَةٌ treatment |
| تَسَمَّمَ [5s] to poison | حائِرٌ bewildered |
| كَوْنٌ (أَكْوانٌ) universe | وَضَّحَ (تَوْضيحٌ) [2s] to clear up |
| طَيَّةٌ fold, pleat | |

*p. 49*

| | |
|---|---|
| في وَقْتٍ لاحِقٍ later | سَهِرَ (سَهَرٌ) [1s4] to stay up, spend the night |
| بارَكَ [3s] to bless | قَلْبٌ (قُلوبٌ) heart |
| صَوابٌ mind; correct | تَوَقَّعَ [5s] to expect |
| عَهِدَ (عَهْدٌ) [1s4] to witness | في ظِلِّ under the guise of |
| مُتَفاجِئٌ surprised | حَذَّرَ مِنْ [2s] to warn of |
| سُرْعَةٌ speed | |
| ذَرَفَ (ذَرْفٌ) [1s2] to shed | |

| | |
|---|---|
| دَفْنٌ (أَدْفانٌ) burial, burying; funeral | أَخْطَرُ more dangerous |
| عِتابٌ repentance; reproach, admonishment | تَوَسَّلَ إلى [5s] to beg, implore |
| مَهْووسٌ بِـ infatuated/obsessed with | تَسَرُّعٌ haste |
| | أَشْفَقَ عَلى [4s] to feel sorry for, take pity on |

## Translation

*p. 42*

Within moments, Romeo's love for Rosaline faded so that Juliet's love, which robbed him of his mind and thoughts, could take its place. He found himself incapable of thinking of anything else but her.

Juliet, that beautiful girl who is supposedly to be his archenemy... he'd fallen in love with her. When and how will he tell her about his longing and yearning? What about her feelings? Is she feeling the same? Does she love him? And if she loves him, how and where will they meet away from the eyes of people? All of these questions were on Romeo's...

*p. 43*

lovesick, confused mind. Perhaps they were also tormenting Juliet's mind... Who knows?

But love sent them a load of strength and steadfastness, and in accordance with time and perhaps with fate, the lovers were given the opportunity to meet again, and what a generous opportunity! It erased all the obstacles and risks the young lovers faced, albeit only for a short period of time.

On their way out of Capulet's palace, Romeo moved away from Benvolio and Mercutio and hid in the dark out of their sight. They tried hard to search for him but to no avail. Mercutio looked at Benvolio and said to him, surprised, "Come on, Benvolio, let's get out of here... He's gone."

"You are right, Mercutio. What is the point in looking for him if he does not want us to find him? Let's go," Benvolio answered him.

They returned home tired from the party.

ക ക ക

In the meantime, Romeo sneaked to the house of Capulet and hid in the shrubs...

*p. 44*

under Juliet's balcony without her noticing his presence.

He spotted his beloved and said to himself, "What is this light that appears from her balcony? Is that my love? Yes, it is she. Oh, if she knew how much I love her... how much I think of her... how much I miss her! How beautiful she is! How tender! Oh! How much I love her! I wish I could touch her glowing cheeks! Please, speak! Speak, bright angel!"

At this time, Juliet was in her room. Her heart was beating with love and longing for Romeo. She stood on her balcony, speaking to herself, unaware of his presence. "Romeo, darling! Why do you have to bear this name? Why don't you strip yourself of your name and your family? Why don't you change your name? Why? Or... if you do not want to change your name, it is enough if you tell me that you love me so that I can forget that I was once from the Capulet family. You are not my enemy; your name is my enemy! Therefore, you won't change if you change your name. So what's keeping you from changing it? You are able to change it, please, change it. What is the importance of names? They never signify what they name. The thing we call a rose would smell just as sweet if we called it by any other name. Please, my beloved Romeo, discard this name and take me instead."

*p. 45*

Romeo listened to every word Juliet uttered. He gathered up his strength, slowly approached her balcony, and spoke to her. "I trust you, my love, and I trust every word you said. I just ask you to tell me if you love me, and I will borrow another name instead of my name. I will not be Romeo Montague anymore!"

Juliet jumped up in alarm and said nervously, "Who is here? Who are you? And what are you doing here at my balcony? And how did you sneak in here? Why were you hiding in the dark and listening to my thoughts?"

"I do not know how I will make myself known. I hate my name; my name is your enemy!" Romeo replied.

"Romeo? Romeo Montague?" Juliet asked him in astonishment and amazement.

"No, I'm not a Romeo, nor a Montague, if you hate them."

Juliet remembered the words she had said from the time she started speaking to herself, and she blushed and asked him, "How did you manage to climb up to my balcony? Climbing the wall is very difficult. How did you do that?"

*p. 46*

Romeo replied with pride, "Your love has given me wings to fly wherever I want."

He went closer to her balcony, and they continued talking about their love and revealing their secrets to each other. They were sure that this love may be a threat to them and that this relationship may end with the death of Romeo if someone discovered it,but Romeo was ready to face death and fight for Juliet. He tried to convince her of the simplicity of the matter, and he reassured her promising love and loyalty to her. And thus he calmed down her fear and hesitation.

Before she said goodbye to him, she begged him to keep his promise and remain faithful to her and to think about her until they met again.

Romeo expressed his deep sadness at leaving her, saying: "What a beautiful encounter, my love!" I fear that this will be a dream I will wake up to face a bitter reality! This meeting is too wonderful to be true. Suddenly, Juliet heard her nanny calling her from inside, so she quickly answered Romeo, "My beloved Romeo, if you really love me and if your intentions are really good and you want me to be your wife, I will send you a messenger tomorrow, and you can pass on a message telling me where and when…

*p. 47*

we'll get married, and I promise to leave everything behind me and follow you."

"My lady!" The nanny cried out again for Juliet.

"Coming! Coming!" Juliet replied.

When will I send him to you? Juliet asked her beloved.

"At nine o'clock," replied Romeo.

They sorrowfully said goodbye to each other in the hope of meeting soon, and Juliet hurried inside. Her home seemed to her like a prison in which she was compelled to live and to obey to the rules of its inhabitants. As for Romeo, he returned to his place, and his heart filled with sadness.

૭૦ ૭૦ ૭૦

It was dawn and hours began to go on and on like years were passing by. Her separation was far more difficult than he had imagined.

Romeo remembered the priest Lawrence, so he

quickly headed for him hoping he could marry them in secret.

The priest Lawrence was holding a basket, engrossed in collecting herbs...

*p. 48*

and flowers. He was praising nature, and its beauty, and endowment, holding a flower in his hand. He said to himself, "Within this tiny flower lies a lethal poison, and at the same time, there is an effective cure. If you smell it, you will feel a wonderful sensation running through your body that will heal you from every illness. But if you taste it, it will certainly poison you and kill you! Everything in this universe has two opposite elements, exactly like man; he carries in himself good and evil together..."

Romeo interrupted the priest's train of though and greeted him. Lawrence asked him, incredulous, "Romeo? What are you doing here, and why you are up at this early hour? Haven't you slept yet? Have you been with Rosaline?"

"Rosaline? No! I've forgotten her, Father!"

"So, where have you been?" Lawrence asked him.

"I was in the house of my enemies. I was celebrating with them. I fell in love... I fell into its trap and I was seriously wounded, Father, and no one can heal me except you!"

Lawrence seemed confused, so he asked Romeo for an explanation. So, he replied, "I love Juliet, the daughter of Lord Capulet. She also...

*p. 49*

loves me. I will tell you later about when, where, and how we met, but now it is important that you declare us husband and wife and bless our marriage."

Father Lawrence nearly lost his mind at this news because he had witnessed Romeo crying daily over Rosaline. He replied, surprised, "What?! And so quickly have you forgotten her and her love? How many tears have you shed for her? How many nights did you cry over her? What happened to you, my son? How quickly you have fallen for someone else! But you are right... Young men love with their eyes and not with their hearts, so do not expect girls to be sincere toward you while you are betraying them!"

"Are you not the one who warned me against Rosaline and her love? Are you not the one who encouraged me to forget her and bury her love, Father?" Romeo asked him in repentance and sorrow.

"My son! I did not ask you to bury a love to find you obsessed with another new love... harsher and more dangerous than the first!"

"Please, Father, help me! I beg you to help us. Make us husband and wife. I really love her and she loves me, too!"

Father Lawrence was never convinced of Romeo's haste, but he felt sorry for him...

*p. 50*

He promised him to secretly marry them.

# اَلْفَصْلُ الرَّابِعُ

مَعَ بُزُوغِ الشَّمْسِ وَبِدَايَةِ يَوْمٍ جَدِيدٍ، اِكْتَشَفَ بَنْفُولْيو وَمَرْكُوشْيو أَنَّ رُومْيو قَدْ قَضَّى لَيْلَتَهُ خَارِجًا وَأَنَّهُ لَمْ يَعُدْ بَعْدُ إِلَى مَنْزِلِهِ. كَانَا يَظُنَّانِ أَنَّهُ لَا يَزَالُ جَزِينًا عَلَى رُوزَالَايْن وَأَنَّهُ لَا يَزَالُ يُفَكِّرُ فِيهَا...

نَظَرَ بَنْفُولْيو إِلَى مَرْكُوشْيو وَسَأَلَهُ: "أَتَعْلَمُ يَا مَرْكُوشْيو أَنَّ تَيْبَالْتْ، قَرِيبُ السَّيِّدِ كَابُولِيتْ، قَدْ أَرْسَلَ رِسَالَةً إِلَى مَنْزِلِ رُومْيو؟"

"لَا بُدَّ مِنْ أَنَّهَا رِسَالَةُ تَحَدِّي!" أَجَابَهُ مَرْكُوشْيو وَوَاصَلَ قَائِلًا: "يَا لَهُ مِنْ مِسْكِينٍ رُومْيو! أَلَا يَكْفِيهِ عَنَاؤُهُ وَحُزْنُهُ؟ أَتُرَاهُ قَادِرٌ عَلَى مُوَاجَهَةِ

قَسْوَةِ وَبَسَالَةِ ذَلِكَ الْمُقَاتِلِ الْمِغْوَارِ تِيبَالْتْ؟ لَا أَظُنُّ ذَلِكَ! فَتِيبَالْتُ قَادِرٌ عَلَى تَحْوِيلِ مُشَادَّةٍ كَلَامِيَّةٍ بَسِيطَةٍ إِلَى مَعْرَكَةٍ دَامِيَّةٍ! إِنَّهُ حَقًّا عَنِيفٌ..." وَلَمْ يَكَدْ مَرْكُوشْيُو يُنْهِي كَلَامَهُ حَتَّى لَمَحَ رُومْيُو يَقْتَرِبُ مِنْهُمَا.

بَدَا رُومْيُو شَاحِبَ اللَّوْنِ وَنَحِيفًا أَكْثَرَ مِنَ الْعَادَةِ. كَمَا بَدَا عَلَيْهِ أَيْضًا الْإِرْهَاقُ وَالْحُزْنُ، غَيْرَ أَنَّ هَذَا لَمْ يَمْنَعْ مَرْكُوشْيُو مِنْ مُعَاتَبَتِهِ عَلَى اخْتِفَائِهِ الْمُرِيبِ لِلَّيْلَةِ السَّابِقَةِ. فَاعْتَذَرَ لَهُمَا مُؤَكِّدًا أَنَّهُ قَدِ انْشَغَلَ بِمَسْأَلَةٍ مُهِمَّةٍ لِلْغَايَةِ. فَرَدَّ عَلَيْهِ مَرْكُوشْيُو مُدَاعِبًا: "أَتَعْنِي أَنَّكَ كُنْتَ مَشْغُولًا تُمَارِسُ الرَّذِيلَةَ؟ أَجِبْنِي! أَلَسْتُ مُحِقًّا؟"

"هَذِهِ مُزْحَةٌ ثَقِيلَةٌ وَغَيْرُ مُضْحِكَةٍ، أَوْ بِالْأَحْرَى فَهِيَ مُزْحَةٌ سَافِلَةٌ يَا مَرْكُوشْيُو!" أَجَابَهُ رُومْيُو.

وَسُرْعَانَ مَا شَرَعَا فِي تَبَادُلِ النِّكَاتِ وَالطَّرَائِفِ الْبَذِيئَةِ، بَيْنَمَا كَانَ بِنْفُولْيُو يُحَاوِلُ إِسْكَاتَهُمَا وَإِنْهَاءَ الْمَهْزَلَةِ. وَظَلُّوا هَكَذَا إِلَى أَنْ لَمَحَ رُومْيُو مُرَبِّيَةَ جُولِييتْ تَقْتَرِبُ مِنْهُمْ وَبِرِفْقَتِهَا الْخَادِمُ بِيتَرْ. فَتَنَفَّسَ رُومْيُو الصُّعَدَاءَ وَهَمَسَ لِنَفْسِهِ قَائِلًا: "إِنَّهَا لَأَخْبَارٌ سَعِيدَةٌ!"

"بَلْ إِنَّهَا لَسَفِينَةٌ عَظِيمَةٌ! إِنَّهَا سَفِينَةٌ! إِنَّهَا سَفِينَةٌ تَقْتَرِبُ مِنَّا!" صَاحَ

بَنْفُولْيُو مُسْتَهْزِأً بِالْمُرَبِّيَةِ الْبَدِينَةِ، وَانْضَمَّ إِلَيْهِ مَرْكُوشْيُو سَاخِرًا مِنَ الْمُرَبِّيَةِ الَّتِي حَاوَلَتْ جَاهِدَةً أَنْ تَتَمَالَكَ أَعْصَابَهَا.

وَأَخِيرًا تَجَاهَلَتْهُمَا وَتَوَجَّهَتْ بِالْكَلَامِ إِلَى رُومْيُو: "أُرِيدُ التَّحَدُّثَ إِلَيْكَ عَلَى انْفِرَادٍ رُومْيُو!" فَاسْتَجَابَ لَهَا هَذَا الْأَخِيرُ وَابْتَعَدَا عَنْ بَنْفُولْيُو وَمَرْكُوشْيُو اللَّذَانِ ذَهَبَا بِدَوْرِهِمَا لِلْغَدَاءِ فِي مَنْزِلِ رُومْيُو.

عَبَّرَتِ الْمُرَبِّيَةُ الْمِسْكِينَةُ عَنْ غَضَبِهَا الشَّدِيدِ تُجَاهَ مَرْكُوشْيُو فَحَاوَلَ رُومْيُو تَهْدِأَتَهَا وَأَخْبَرَهَا أَنَّهُ كَانَ فَقَطْ يَمْزَحُ.

لَمْ تَبْدُ الْمُرَبِّيَةُ مُقْتَنِعَةً كَثِيرًا وَلَكِنَّهَا قَالَتْ لَهُ: "حَسَنًا، حَسَنًا، لَا بَأْسَ. لَقَدْ أَرْسَلَتْنِي آنِسَتِي إِلَيْكَ وَلَكِنْ يَا رُومْيُو، اسْتَمِعْ إِلَيَّ جَيِّدًا! إِنْ كُنْتَ سَتَعْبَثُ بِهَا وَبِمَشَاعِرِهَا فَعَلَيْكَ أَنْ تَبْتَعِدَ عَنْهَا فِي الْحَالِ، وَإِيَّاكَ أَنْ تَقْتَرِبَ مِنْهَا! فَآنِسَتِي لَا زَالَتْ صَغِيرَةَ السِّنِّ وَرَقِيقَةَ الْمَشَاعِرِ، وَلَنْ تَتَحَمَّلَ أَيَّ وَجَعٍ. فَإِيَّاكَ أَنْ تُؤْذِيهَا أَوْ تَخْذِلَهَا! أَهَذَا مَفْهُومٌ؟"

"كُونِي عَلَى يَقِينٍ أَنَّنِي أَبَدًا لَنْ أُؤْذِيهَا! وَأَرْجُوكِ قَوْلِي لَهَا أَنْ تُخَطِّطَ لِلْهُرُوبِ مِنَ الْمَنْزِلِ كَيْ نَلْتَقِيَ فِي حُجْرَةِ الْقِسِّيسِ لُورِنْس وَنَعْتَرِفَ لَهُ... ثُمَّ يُزَوِّجُنَا سِرًّا" أَجَابَهَا رُومْيُو مُقَدِّمًا لَهَا نُقُودًا كَمُكَافَأَةٍ لَهَا.

وَبَعْدَ تَرَدُّدٍ، أَخَذَتِ الْمُرَبِّيَةُ النُّقودَ وَتَرَجَّاها روميو أَنْ تَظَلَّ مُخْلِصَةً لَهُما.

مَعَ مُنْتَصَفِ النَّهارِ، بَدَأَتْ جولييت تَقْلَقُ، فَالْمُرَبِّيَةُ لَمْ تَعُدْ بَعْدُ.

"لِمَ لَمْ تَأْتِ بَعْدُ يا تُرى؟ لَقَدْ أَرْسَلْتُها مُنْذُ ثَلاثِ ساعاتٍ! أَيْنَ هِيَ يا تُرى؟ مِنَ الْمُفْتَرَضِ أَنْ يَكونَ رَسولُ الْحُبِّ خَفيفًا سَريعًا... وَلَيْسَ ثَقيلًا بَطيئًا هٰكَذا! رُبَّما لَمْ تَجِدْهُ!؟" كانَتْ مُضْطَرِبَةً وَتَنْتَظِرُ الْمُرَبِّيَةَ بِفارِغِ الصَّبْرِ، وَبَدَتْ لَها الدَّقائِقُ وَالثَّواني وَكَأَنَّها ساعاتٌ... إِلى أَنْ لَمَحَتْ أَخيرًا مُرَبِّيَتَها وَبيتر يَقْتَرِبانِ شَيْئًا فَشَيْئًا، فَهَرَعَتْ صَوْبَهُما وَقَدْ كادَتْ تَفْقِدُ صَبْرَها. أَرْسَلَتِ الْمُرَبِّيَةُ بيتر بَعيدًا عَنْهُما وَانْفَرَدَتْ بِجولييت، وَجَلَسَتْ في إِرْهاقٍ تَلْتَقِطُ أَنْفاسَها.

"أَرْجوكِ تَكَلَّمي، ماذا قالَ لَكِ؟" قالَتْ لَها جولييت مُتَوَسِّلَةً.

"اِنْتَظِري، فَأَنا الْآنَ مُتْعَبَةٌ جِدًّا! دَعيني أَرْتاحُ قَليلًا، عِظامي تُؤْلِمُني" أَجابَتْها الْمُرَبِّيَةُ.

"لَيْتَكِ تَسْتَطيعينَ أَخْذَ عِظامي! هَيّا أَرْجوكِ تَكَلَّمي!"

"لِمَ أَنتِ عَلَى عَجَلَةٍ مِنْ أَمْرِكِ؟ لِمَ؟ أَلَا تَسْتَطِيعِينَ أَنْ تَصْبِرِي قَلِيلًا؟ أَلَا تَرَيْنَ أَنَّنِي بِالْكَادِ أَتَنَفَّسُ؟"

"حَسَنًا، قُولِي لِي أَرْجُوكِ، هَلِ الْأَخْبَارُ سَعِيدَةٌ أَمْ حَزِينَةٌ؟"

وَبَعْدَ أَنْ جَعَلَتْ جُولِييت تَنْتَظِرُ دَهْرًا، نَطَقَتِ الْمُرَبِّيَةُ أَخِيرًا: "حَسَنًا، يُمْكِنُنِي الْقَوْلُ أَنَّكِ لَمْ تُحْسِنِي الِاخْتِيَارَ... مَعَ أَنَّهُ شَابٌّ وَسِيمٌ وَجَذَّابٌ، إِلَّا أَنَّهُ لَيْسَ مُهَذَّبًا كَثِيرًا... وَلَكِنْ لَا بَأْسَ! فَهُوَ وَدِيعٌ كَالْجَمَلِ، صَدِّقِينِي آنِسَتِي! لِهَذَا، أَنتِ حُرَّةٌ، افْعَلِي مَا تَشَائِينَ! قُولِي لِي أَرْجُوكِ، هَلْ تَنَاوَلْتِ الْفُطُورَ؟"

"لَا!" رَدَّتْ جُولِييت بِتَشَنُّجٍ، "لَمْ أَتَنَاوَلْ فُطُورِي، وَمَا الْجَدِيدُ فِي كُلِّ مَا أَخْبَرْتِنِي بِهِ لِتَوِّكِ؟ أَخْبِرِينِي مَاذَا قَالَ لَكِ رُومْيُو عَنَّا وَعَنْ زَوَاجِنَا؟ أَخْبِرِينِي أَرْجُوكِ"

"حَسَنًا، إِنَّ حَبِيبَكِ الْوَسِيمَ قَالَ لِي... آنِسَتِي! أَيْنَ وَالِدَتُكِ؟"

"وَالِدَتِي؟ مَا دَخْلُ وَالِدَتِي فِي هَذَا الْمَوْضُوعِ؟ إِنَّهَا فِي الدَّاخِلِ! أَرْجُوكِ أَخْبِرِينِي مَاذَا قَالَ لَكِ حَبِيبِي رُومْيُو!"

"حَسَنًا، حَسَنًا، اهْدَئِي وَقُولِي لِي، هَلْ تَسْتَطِيعِينَ أَنْ تَسْتَأْذِنِي

عائِلَتِكِ لِتَذْهَبي الْيَوْمَ وَتَعْتَرِفي إِلَى الْكاهِنِ؟"

"نَعَمْ."

"مُمْتازٌ! إِذَنْ أَسْرِعي إِلَى حَبيبِكِ رومْيو، فَهُوَ في انْتِظارِكِ عِنْدَ جِدارِ حُجْرَةِ الْكاهِنِ لورِنْسْ." اِحْمَرَّتْ وَجْنَتا جولِييتْ فَرَحًا وَخَجَلًا، في حينِ واصَلَتِ الْمُرَبِّيَةُ كَلامَها: "هَيّا اذْهَبي إِلَى الْكَنيسَةِ الْآنَ حَيْثُ سَيُزَوِّجُكُما الْكاهِنُ. أَمّا أَنا، فَسَأُحْضِرُ سُلَّمًا لِيَتَسَلَّقَهُ رومْيو كَيْ يَصِلَ إِلَيْكِ عَبْرَ الْجِدارِ."

"حَسَنًا مُرَبِّيَتي الْعَزيزَةُ! تَمَنَّيْ لي حَظًّا سَعيدًا! شُكْرًا لَكِ! إِلَى اللِّقاءِ!" أَجابَتْها جولِييتْ وَقَدْ كادَتْ تَطيرُ فَرَحًا.

"إِلَى اللِّقاءِ" رَدَّتِ الْمُرَبِّيَةُ.

في هَذِهِ الْأَثْناءِ، وَصَلَ رومْيو إِلَى الْقِسّيسِ لورِنْسْ وَبَقِيا يَنْتَظِرانِ وُصولَ جولِييتْ.

"لِيُبارِكِ اللَّهُ قِرانَكُما وَيُسْعِدَكُما وَلِيَحْميكُما مِنْ كُلِّ مَكْروهٍ قَدْ يَطْرَأُ!" قالَ لورِنْسْ لِرومْيو. "مَكْروهٌ؟ لا يَهُمُّني ذَلِكَ! يَكْفيني حُبُّ جولِييتْ،

فَأنا لا أَهْتَمُّ لِشَيْءٍ سِوَى لِحُبِّها وإنْ أَصابَني مَكْروهٌ... فَيَكْفي أَنَّها سَتُصْبِحُ زَوْجَتي!" أجابَهُ روميو مُتَحَمِّسًا.

"كَفاكَ مُبالَغَةً يا بُنَيَّ! فَالْحُبُّ وَالْحَياةُ الزَّوْجِيَّةُ لا يَسْتَمِرّانِ إلَّا بِالِاعْتِدالِ..."

وَفي هَذِهِ اللَّحْظَةِ، دَخَلَتْ عَلَيْهِما جولييت مَهْرولَةً، وَارْتَمَتْ في أَحْضانِ روميو في اشْتِياقٍ، وَظَلَّا يَتَبادَلانِ الْقُبَلَ وَكَلِماتِ الْحُبِّ إلى أَنْ قاطَعَهُما الْقِسِّيسُ لورِنْس قائِلًا: "هَيَّا لِنَعْقِدَ هَذا الْقِرانَ وَلِأُبارِكَ زَواجَكُما!"

رَكَعَ روميو وجولييت أَمامَ الْقِسِّيسِ في حينِ شَرَعَ هَذا الْأَخيرُ في عَقْدِ قِرانِهِما وَبارَكَ زَواجَهُما.

# Vocabulary

### p. 63

| | |
|---|---|
| قَضَى [2d] to spend (time) | تَحَدٍّ challenge |
| حَزِينٌ (حُزَنَاءُ) sad | مِسْكِينٌ (مَسَاكِينُ) poor (fellow) |
| لَا بُدَّ مِنْ أَنْ must | أَتُرَاهُ I wonder if he... |

### p. 64

| | |
|---|---|
| بَسَالَةٌ valor, bravery, boldness | اِنْشَغَلَ بِ [7s] to be busy with |
| مُقَاتِلٌ fighter, warrior | مَسْأَلَةٌ (مَسَائِلُ) issue, question |
| مِغْوَارٌ (مَغَاوِيرُ) fighting; courageous, bold | مُدَاعِبًا joking, in jest |
| | مَارَسَ [3s] to practice |
| حَوَّلَ (تَحْوِيلٌ) [2s] to turn, change | رَذِيلَةٌ (رَذَائِلُ) depravity |
| مُشَادَّةٌ altercation, quarrel | مُحِقٌّ (in the) right |
| دَامٍ bloody | مُضْحِكٌ funny |
| أَنْهَى [4d] to finish | بِالْأَحْرَى rather, but |
| شَاحِبٌ pale | طُرْفَةٌ (طَرَائِفُ) joke |
| نَحِيفٌ (نُحَفَاءُ) thin, skinny | بَذِيءٌ obscene |
| إِرْهَاقٌ exhaustion | أَسْكَتَ (إِسْكَاتٌ) [4s] to silence |
| عَاتَبَ (مُعَاتَبَةٌ) [3s] to reproach | أَنْهَى (إِنْهَاءٌ) ending |
| اِخْتِفَاءٌ disappearance | مَهْزَلَةٌ (مَهَازِلُ) farce |
| مُرِيبٌ suspicious | تَنَفَّسَ [5s] to breathe |
| سَابِقَةٌ preceding | صُعَدَاءُ deep sigh |
| اِعْتَذَرَ [8s1] to apologize | هَمَسَ (هَمْسٌ) [1s2] to whisper |
| مُؤَكَّدٌ confirming | سَفِينَةٌ (سُفُنٌ) ship |

## p. 65

| | |
|---|---|
| ساخِرٌ مِن mocking | إِيَّاكَ أَنْ don't you dare... |
| تَمالَكَ [6s] to keep in check | تَحَمَّلَ [5s] to bear, endure |
| عَصَبٌ (أَعْصابٌ) nerve | وَجَعٌ (أَوْجاعٌ) ache, pain |
| أَخيرًا finally | آذَى [4d(a)] to hurt, harm |
| تَوَجَّهَ [5s] to head for | خَذَلَ (خِذْلانٌ) [1s3] to disappoint |
| عَلَى انْفِرادٍ privately, alone | مَفْهومٌ (مَفاهيمُ) understood |
| اِسْتَجابَ لِ [10h] to respond to | خَطَّطَ [2s] to plan |
| غَداءٌ lunch | هُروبٌ escape |
| تُجاهَ towards | حُجْرَةٌ (حُجَرٌ) cell; room |
| مَزَحَ (مُزاحٌ/مَزْحٌ) [1s1] to joke | اِعْتَرَفَ [8s1] to confess, acknowledge |
| بَدا (بُدُوٌّ) [1d3] to appear, seem | مُقَدَّمًا in advance |
| آنِسَتي my lady | نُقودٌ pl. money |
| جَيِّدًا well | مُكافَأَةٌ (مُكافَآتٌ) reward, award |
| عَبِثَ بِ (عَبَثٌ) [1s4] to abuse | |

## p. 66

| | |
|---|---|
| ظَلَّ (ظَلَّ) [1g1] to remain, continue to be | اِنْفَرَدَ بِ [7s] to be alone with |
| مُنْتَصَفٌ middle, mid- | اِلْتَقَطَ [8s1] to collect, gather |
| قَلِقَ (قَلَقٌ) [1s4] to worry | مُتَوَسِّلٌ begging |
| خَفيفٌ (خِفافٌ) light | وَدَعَ (وَدْعٌ) [1a1] to let, leave: |
| بَطيءٌ slow | دَعيني imperative let me... |
| مُضْطَرِبٌ nervous, anxious | اِرْتاحَ [8h1] to relax |
| بِفارِغِ الصَّبْرِ impatiently | عَظْمٌ (عِظامٌ) bone |
| دَقيقَةٌ (دَقائِقُ) minute | آلَمَ [4s(a)] to hurt, cause pain |
| فَقَدَ (فِقْدانٌ/فَقْدٌ) [1s2] to lose | لَيْتَ + pronoun suffix if only |
| | اِسْتَطاعَ [10h] to be able to |

## p. 67

| | |
|---|---|
| عَجَلَةٌ hurry, haste | صَبَرَ (صَبْرٌ) [1s2] to be patient |

| | |
|---|---|
| بِالْكَادِ barely | (حُمْلان) حَمَلٌ lamb |
| دَهْرًا a long time | صَدَّقَ [2s] to believe |
| (نُطْقٌ) [1s3] نَطَقَ to utter, say | تَنَاوَلَ [6s] to consume, eat |
| أَمْكَنَ [4s] to be possible (for) | فُطورٌ breakfast |
| أَحْسَنَ [4s] to do well | تَشَنُّجٌ tremble, quiver, spasm |
| اِخْتِيَارٌ choosing, selection | لِتَوِّك just (now) |
| جَذَّابٌ attractive | اِسْتَأْذَنَ [10s(a)] to be excused from, get away from |
| وَديعٌ gentle, docile | |

*p. 68*

| | |
|---|---|
| (كَهَنَةٌ) كَاهِنٌ priest | تَسَلَّقَ [5s] to climb |
| اِنْتِظَارٌ waiting | عَبَرَ over, across |
| (جُدْرانٌ) جِدارٌ wall | تَمَنَّى [5d] to wish, hope |
| (أَفْراحٌ) فَرَحٌ delight, glee, joy, happiness | وُصولٌ arrival |
| حَيْثُ where | قِرانٌ marriage, wedding |
| (إِحْضَارٌ) [4s] أَحْضَرَ to bring, fetch | أَسْعَدَ [4s] to help; make happy |
| (سَلالِمٌ) سُلَّمٌ ladder | (طَرْءٌ) [1s1(b)] طَرَأَ to happen, befall |

*p. 69*

| | |
|---|---|
| اِهْتَمَّ [8g1] to be interested | اِرْتَمَى [8d1] to be thrown, throw oneself |
| مُبالَغَةٌ exaggeration | (أَحْضانٌ) حِضْنٌ bosom; *here: pl.* arms, embrace |
| زَوْجيٌّ marital | (عَقْدٌ) [1s2] عَقَدَ to tie, bind |
| اِسْتَمَرَّ [10g] to continue | (رُكوعٌ) [1s1] رَكَعَ to kneel |
| اِعْتِدالٌ moderation | |

## Translation

*p. 63*

As the sun rose and a new day began, Benvolio and Mercutio discovered that Romeo had spent his night out and that he was not yet home. They thought he was still sad about Rosaline and that he was still thinking about her.

"Benvolio looked at Mercutio and asked him, "Do you know, Mercutio, that Tybalt, a relative of Lord Capulet, has sent a letter to Romeo's house?"

"It must be a challenge letter!" Mercutio replied, "Poor Romeo! Are his weariness and grief not enough for him? I wonder if he is capable of confronting…

*p. 64*

the cruelty and bravery of Tybalt, that fierce fighter? I do not think so! Tybalt is able to turn a simple verbal argument into a bloody battle! He is really violent…" Mercutio had not yet finished what he was saying when he saw Romeo approaching them.

Romeo looked pale and skinnier than usual. He also seemed tired and sad, but this did not prevent Mercutio from reproaching him about his mysterious disappearance the night before. Romeo apologized to them, confirming that he was preoccupied with a very important issue.

Mercutio replied jokingly, "Do you mean you were busy lusting? Answer me! Am I not right?"

"That is not at all funny; rather, it's a very mean joke, Mercutio!" Romeo answered him.

They soon began to share obscene jokes while Benvolio tried to silence them and end the comedy. They remained so until Juliet's nanny approached them, accompanied by the servant Peter. Romeo sighed and whispered to himself, "It's good news!"

"It is a huge ship! It's a ship! It's a ship approaching us!" Benvolio yelled...

*p. 65*

at the fat nanny mockingly, and Mercutio joined him while the nanny tried hard to keep calm.

Finally, she ignored them and went to speak to Romeo, "I want to talk to you privately, Romeo!" He responded to her and moved away from Benvolio and Mercutio, who went to lunch at Romeo's house.

The poor nanny expressed her anger at Mercutio, and Romeo tried to calm her down and told her that he was just joking.

The nanny did not seem too convinced, but she said: "Very well, never mind. My lady sent me to you, but listen to me well, Romeo! If you intend to play with her feelings, you should move away from her immediately and you should never approach her! My lady is still young and very sensitive and won't be able to stand being hurt. Don't you dare hurt her or let her down! Is this understood?"

"Be sure, I will never hurt her! And tell her to plan to escape from the house so that we meet in the cell of Friar Lawrence. We'll confess to him, and then he'll marry us in secret," Romeo replied while giving her money as a reward....

*p. 66*

After hesitation, the nanny took the money, and Romeo begged her to remain loyal to them.

୨୦ ୨୦ ୨୦

By midday, Juliet began to worry that the nanny hadn't come yet.

"Why has she not come yet? I sent her three hours ago! Where is she? The messenger of love is supposed to be light and fast... not so slow! Maybe she did not find him!?" She was nervous and waited impatiently for the nanny. The minutes and seconds seemed to her like hours. Finally, she noticed the nanny approaching slowly with Peter. She ran toward them, almost losing her patience. The nanny sent Peter away from them and remained alone with Juliet. She sat in exhaustion to catch her breath.

"Please tell me, what did he say to you?" Juliet begged her.

"Wait, I'm now very tired! Let me rest a little; my bones hurt," the nanny replied.

"If only you could take my bones! Come on, please tell!"

*p. 67*

"Why you are in a hurry? Why? Can't you be patient a little? Don't you see that I can barely breathe?"

"Well, tell me, please, is it happy or sad news?"

After making Juliet wait so long, the nanny finally said, "Well, I can say that you did not make a very good choice. Although he is handsome and attractive, he is not very polite... but never mind! He is gentle like a lamb, believe me, miss! So, you are free; do whatever you want! But tell me, did you have breakfast?"

"No!" Juliet answered nervously, "I did not have my

breakfast, and what's new in what you just told me? Tell me what Romeo told you about us and about our marriage? Please tell me!"

"Well, your handsome lover told me... My lady, where is your mother?"

"My mother? What does my mother have to do with this? She's inside! Please tell me what my beloved Romeo said to you!"

"Well, well, calm down and tell me, can you escape...

*p. 68*

from your family today and go to the priest for a confession?"

"Yes."

"Excellent! So go to your beloved Romeo. He is waiting for you at the wall of Friar Lawrence's cell." Juliet was blushing and embarrassed, while the nanny continued, "Go to the church now where the priest will marry you. As for me, I will bring a ladder for Romeo to climb in order to reach you over the wall."

"Very well, my dear nanny! Wish me good luck! Thank you! Goodbye!" Juliet answered her and was very happy.

"Goodbye!" The nanny answered.

৩৯ ৩৯ ৩৯

In the meantime, Romeo arrived at Friar Lawrence's and waited for Juliet's arrival.

"May God bless and grant you good health and protect you from all evil that may happen," Lawrence told Romeo. "Evil? I do not care! Juliet's love is enough...

*p. 69*

I do not care for anything but her love even if I get hurt. It is enough that she will become my wife!" Romeo replied enthusiastically.

"Enough exaggeration, my son! Love and marital life only go on in moderation."

At this moment, Juliet entered and ran into Romeo's arms longingly. They exchanged kisses and words of love until Friar Lawrence interrupted them, "Let's make you husband and wife, and let me bless your marriage"

Romeo and Juliet knelt in front of the priest while he began to join them in matrimony and bless their marriage.

# اَلْفَصْلُ الْخَامِسُ

كانَ الْجَوُّ شَديدَ الْحَرارَةِ وَمَرْكوشيو يُحاوِلُ أَنْ يُقْنِعَ بَنْفوليو بِالْخُروجِ، إِلَّا أَنَّ هَذا الْأَخيرَ لَمْ تَكُنْ لَدَيْهِ أَيُّ رَغْبَةٍ في ذَلِكَ.

"مَرْكوشيو أَرْجوكَ! لا أُريدُ التَّجَوُّلَ الْآنَ، فَالطَّقْسُ حارٌّ وَلا أُحِبُّ أَنْ أَتَشاجَرَ مَعَ أَحَدٍ مِنْ عائِلَةِ كابوليت... فَالْحَرارَةُ كَما تَعْرِفُ تَجْعَلُ الْإِنْسانَ يَفْقِدُ أَعْصابَهُ سَريعًا وَيَميلُ إِلَى الشِّجارِ وَالْعُنْفِ!"

فَرَدَّ عَلَيْهِ مَرْكوشيو في سُخْرِيَّةٍ: "تَتَكَلَّمُ وَكَأَنَّ الْحَرارَةَ هِيَ فِعْلًا سَبَبُ عُنْفِكَ وَلَكِنَّكَ أَنْتَ في الْحَقيقَةِ عَنيفٌ بِطَبْعِكَ! فَأَنْتَ عَصَبِيٌّ دائِمًا

وَحَتَّى إِنْ غابَتْ كُلُّ أَسْبابِ الشِّجارِ فَأَنْتَ قادِرٌ عَلَى اِخْتِلاقِها وَاِفْتِعالِها كَيْ تَتَشاجَرَ!" وَظَلَّ مَرْكوشْيو هَكَذا يَسْتَفِزُّ بِنْفولْيو مُحاوِلًا إِقْناعَهُ بِالتَّسَكُّعِ قَلِيلًا فِي الْمَدينَةِ، إِلَى أَنْ لَمَحا تَيْبالْتْ يَقْتَرِبُ مِنْهُما بِرِفْقَةِ **بَتْروكْيو** وَرِجالٍ آخَرِينَ مِنْ عائِلَةِ كابولِيت.

"أُرِيدُ التَّحَدُّثَ مَعَ أَحَدِكُما لَوْ سَمَحْتُما"قالَ تَيْبالْتْ مُتَوَجِّهًا بِكَلامِهِ إِلَى مَرْكوشْيو وَبِنْفولْيو وَقَدْ وَقَفَ بَتْروكْيو قَرِيبًا مِنْهُ مُتَوَجِّهًا الْحَذَرَ، وَواصَلَ: "مَرْكوشْيو، أَنْتَ قَرِيبٌ جِدًّا مِنْ رومْيو وَكَثِيرًا ما تَتَسَكَّعانِ مَعًا..." قاطَعَهُ مَرْكوشْيو وَالْغَضَبُ قَدْ تَطايَرَ مِنْ عَيْنَيْهِ: "ماذا قُلْتَ؟ نَتَسَكَّعُ؟ أَلا تَعْرِفُ كَيْفَ تَنْتَقِي كَلِماتَكَ؟ أَتَتَخَيَّلُنا مُوسِيقِيُّونَ مُتَجَوِّلُونَ أَمْ ماذا؟ وَإِنْ كُنْتَ تَظُنُّنا كَذَلِكَ فَسَوْفَ أُسْمِعُكَ موسِيقَى رائِعَةً، سَأَجْعَلُكَ تَرْقُصُ عَلَى أَوْتارِها!" وَأَشارَ إِلَى سِلاحِهِ فِي اِسْتِهْزاءٍ.

اِضْطَرَبَ بِنْفولْيو وَقالَ مُحاوِلًا تَهْدِئَةَ الْأَجْواءِ: "إِنَّنا فِي مَكانٍ عامٍّ يا شَبابُ فَاهْدَآ قَلِيلًا لَوْ سَمَحْتُما وَتَكَلَّما بِرَصانَةٍ وَعَقْلانِيَّةٍ، أَوِ اذْهَبا إِلَى مَكانٍ آخَرَ بَعِيدًا عَنْ أَعْيُنِ النّاسِ."

فَرَدَّ مَرْكوشْيو فِي غُرورٍ: "أَعْيُنُ النّاسِ خُلِقَتْ لِلنَّظَرِ، فَلْيُشاهِدِ الْجَمِيعُ! لَنْ أَتَحَرَّكَ مِنْ هُنا."

وَهُنا الْتَحَقَ بِهِمْ رومْيو، فَنَظَرَ إِلَيْهِ تَيْبالْتْ مُتَوَجِّهًا بِكَلامِهِ إِلَى مَرْكوشْيو: "اِنْتَهَتْ مُهِمَّتُكَ الآنَ، فَالْمَعْنِيُّ الْحَقيقيُّ بِالْأَمْرِ قَدْ وَصَلَ... رومْيو!" قالَ تَيْبالْتْ في حِقْدٍ "أَنْتَ نَذْلٌ!"

فَأَجابَهُ رومْيو بِكُلِّ هُدوءٍ: "تَيْبالْتْ! أَتَعْلَمُ أَنَّ هُناكَ ما يَجْعَلُني أُحِبُّكَ وَأَنْسَى الْحِقْدَ وَالْكَراهِيَةَ الَّتي بَيْنَنا وَأَغْفِرَ لَكَ شَتائِمَكَ؟ أَنا لَسْتُ بِنَذْلٍ يا تَيْبالْتْ... إِلَى اللِّقاءِ!"

"كَلامُكَ هَذا لَنْ يُقْنِعَني وَلَنْ يُصْلِحَ ما فَعَلْتَهُ، فَلِهَذا عُدْ في الْحالِ وَلِنَتخاصَمَ!"

فَرَدَّ رومْيو: "أَنْتَ مُخْطِئٌ يا تَيْبالْتْ! لَمْ أَفْعَلْ لَكَ شَيْئًا.. بَلْ عَلَى الْعَكْسِ... أَنا أُحِبُّكَ أَكْثَرَ مِمَّا تَتَصَوَّرُ. وَسَتَكْتَشِفُ وَحْدَكَ السَّبَبَ، لِهَذا عَلَيْكَ أَنْ تَسْعَدَ بِكَلامي هَذا..."

صُدِمَ مَرْكوشْيو بِجَوابِ رومْيو وَقالَ في ذُهولٍ: "إِنَّ هَذا الْكَلامَ الَّذي تَقولُهُ يا رومْيو لَعارٌ عَلَيْكَ وَعَلَيْنا جَميعًا! سَأُنْهي هَذِهِ الْمَسْأَلَةَ في الْحالِ!" وَأَشْهَرَ سَيْفَهُ في وَجْهِ تَيْبالْتِ الَّذي قَبِلَ التَّحَدِّي.

وَرَغْمَ مُحاوَلاتِ رومْيو لِصَدِّهِما عَنِ الْقِتالِ مُهَدِّدًا إِيّاهُما بِحُضورِ

الْأَمِيرِ، إِلَّا أَنَّهُما تَجاهَلاهُ. وَبَيْنَما هُما يَتَشاجَرانِ ورومْيو واقِفٌ بَيْنَهُما، أَصابَ تَيْبالْتْ مَرْكوشْيو مِنْ تَحْتِ ذِراعِ رومْيو إِصابَةً خَطيرَةً جِدًّا أَوْقَعَتْ بِهِ أَرْضًا مُتَخَبِّطًا في دِمائِهِ.

فَرَّ تَيْبالْتْ وَرِجالُهُ هارِبينَ، في حينِ جَرى خادِمُ مَرْكوشْيو يُفَتِّشُ عَنْ طَبيبٍ لِسَيِّدِهِ. حَمَلَ بَنْفولْيو صَديقَهُ الْمُصابَ إِلَى إِحْدَى الْمَنازِلِ الْقَريبَةِ عَلى أَمَلِ إِنْقاذِهِ بَيْنَما مَرْكوشْيو لَمْ يَكُفَّ عَنْ سَبِّ وَشَتْمِ عائِلَتَيْ مُنْتغْيو وَكابوليت وَاللَّتانِ كانَ بِسَبَبِهِما يَتَأَلَّمُ... وَرُبَّما يُحْتَضَرُ!

ظَلَّ رومْيو مِباكِيًا في مَكانِهِ تَحْتَ تَأْثيرِ الصَّدْمَةِ يُفَكِّرُ: "مِسْكينٌ صَديقي مَرْكوشْيو! سَيَفْقِدُ حَياتَهُ بِسَبَبي... كانَ يُحاوِلُ الدِّفاعَ عَنّي وَحِمايَتي مِنْ تَيْبالْتْ... أَنا الْمُذْنِبُ... أَنا الْمُذْنِبُ..."

قَطَعَ بَنْفولْيو حَبْلَ أَفْكارِهِ مُعْلِنًا لَهُ خَبَرَ وَفاةِ صَديقِهِما وَقَريبِ أَميرِ فيرونا، مَرْكوشْيو! عَلَّقَ رومْيو عَلَى الْخَبَرِ في أَلَمٍ: "هَذا خَبَرٌ مُريعٌ وَبِدايَةٌ لِأَحْداثٍ داميَةٍ سَنَشْهَدُها في الْأَيَّامِ الْمُقْبِلَةِ... وَسَتَنْتَهي بِبَشاعَةٍ!"

وَما أَنْ أَنْهَى كَلامَهُ حَتَّى وَجَدَ تَيْبالْتْ قَدْ عادَ إِلَيْهِ. فَنَظَرَ إِلَيْهِ رومْيو

في حِقْدٍ وَقالَ لَهُ: "آنَ الْأَوانُ لِلْأَثَأْرَ لِنَفْسي وَلِمَرْكوشْيو الَّذي لا تَزالُ روحُهُ تَطوفُ حَوْلَنا وَتَنْتَظِرُ مُلاقاةَ روحِكَ! إلَى الْقِتالِ يا تَيْبالْت! وَأَحَدُنا سَوْفَ يَلْتَحِقُ بِمَرْكوشْيو الْيَوْمَ! إِمَّا أَنا، أَوْ أَنْتَ، أَوْ كِلانا!"

فانْدَفَعَ تَيْبالْت نَحْوَ روميو مُسْتَخِفًّا بِهِ وَبَدآ يَتَشاجَرانِ بِعُنْفٍ. ظَلَّا يَتَخاصَمانِ بِأَسْلِحَتِهِما إلَى أَنْ سَقَطَ تَيْبالْت عَلَى الْأَرْضِ مَغْشِيًّا عَلَيْهِ يَلْفِظُ أَنْفاسَهُ الْأَخيرَةَ تَحْتَ مَرْآى الْمارَّةِ الَّذينَ احْتَشَدوا لِمُشاهَدَةِ ما يَجْري.

وَقَفَ روميو يَنْظُرُ إِلَى جُثَّةِ تَيْبالْت في ذُهولٍ، فَصَرَخَ بِوَجْهِهِ بَنْفوليو: "روميو اذْهَبْ مِنْ هُنا! فَالنَّاسُ قَدْ شَهِدوا عَلَى الْمَعْرَكَةِ، وَالْأَميرُ سَيَحْكُمُ عَلَيْكَ بِالْإِعْدامِ! أَرْجوكَ اذْهَبْ مِنْ هُنا!"

وَصَلَ الْأَميرُ إِلَى مَوْقِعِ الْمَعْرَكَةِ، وَبِرِفْقَتِهِ السَّيِّدُ مُنْتَغْيو وَزَوْجَتُهُ وَالسَّيِّدُ كابوليت وَزَوْجَتُهُ، وَرِجالٌ آخَرونَ. صَرَخَ الْأَميرُ: "آتوني بِكُلِّ مَنْ شارَكَ في هَذِهِ الْعَمَلِيَّةِ الدَّامِيَّةِ حالًا!"

اسْتَجْمَعَ بَنْفوليو قُواهُ وَقالَ: "مَوْلايَ! أَسْتَطيعُ أَنْ أَسْرُدَ لَكُمْ ما حَصَلَ!

هَذا تَيْبَالْتْ مَقْتُولًا... لَقَدْ قَتَلَ أَحَدَ أَقْرِبائِكُمُ الْمُخْلِصِينَ! مَرْكُوشِيُو! ثُمَّ هَرَبَ لِيَعُودَ مُجَدَّدًا إِلَى رُومْيُو وَيَتَشاجَرَ مَعَهُ، فَقَتَلَهُ هَذا الْأَخِيرُ..."

إِنْهارَتِ السَّيِّدَةُ كابُولِيتْ لَدَى رُؤْيَةِ جُثَّةِ تَيْبَالْتْ وَتَوَسَّلَتْ إِلَى الْأَمِيرِ أَنْ يَثْأَرَ لَها وَأَنْ يَقْتُلَ أَحَدَ أَفْرادِ عائِلَةِ مُنْتَغْيُو.

وَأَمامَ حَيْرَةِ الْأَمِيرِ، حاوَلَ بَنْفُولْيُو الدِّفاعَ عَنْ رُومْيُو وَإِقْناعَ الْأَمِيرِ بِبَراءَتِهِ مُواصِلًا: "إِنَّ تَيْبَالْتْ يا مَوْلايَ هُوَ الظَّالِمُ وَهُوَ الَّذِي بَدَأَ الْمَعْرَكَةَ، وَرُومْيُو قَدْ دَعاهُ لِلْهُدوءِ دُونَ جَدْوَى. فَتَشاجَرَ تَيْبَالْتْ مَعَ مَرْكُوشِيُو مُتَجاهِلانِ نَصائِحَ رُومْيُو إِلَى أَنْ سَقَطَ تَيْبَالْتْ قَتِيلًا. ثُمَّ بَعْدَ ذَلِكَ عادَ لِاسْتِفْزازِ رُومْيُو الَّذِي كانَ حَزِينًا عَلَى صَدِيقِنا. وَعِنْدَها... أَخَذَ بِثَأْرِهِ مِنْ تَيْبَالْتْ الْمُتَوَحِّشِ وَقَتَلَهُ... هَذِهِ هِيَ كُلُّ الْحَقِيقَةِ يا مَوْلايَ!"

اِزْدادَتْ حَيْرَةُ الْأَمِيرِ الَّذِي كانَ يُحاوِلُ اِتِّخاذَ قَرارٍ عادِلٍ تُجاهَ الطَّرَفَيْنِ، فِي حِينَ حاوَلَتْ عائِلَةُ كابُولِيتْ الدِّفاعَ عَنِ ابْنِها تَيْبَالْتْ بَيْنَما كانَتْ عائِلَةُ مُنْتَغْيُو تُحاوِلُ إِنْقاذَ مَصِيرِ رُومْيُو. وَبَعْدَ تَرَدُّدٍ طَوِيلٍ نَطَقَ الْأَمِيرُ بِقَرارِهِ الْحاسِمِ: "مِنَ الْيَوْمِ فَصاعِدًا... رُومْيُو مُقْصًى مِنْ مَدِينَةِ فِيرُونا... وَلَنْ يَعُودَ إِلَيْها أَبَدًا! لَقَدْ لَقِيَ قَرِيبِي مَرْكُوشِيُو حَتْفَهُ

جَرَّاءَ عَدَاوَتِكُمْ... فَلْيُغَادِرْ رُومْيُو الْمَدِينَةَ فَوْرًا وَإِلَّا فَسَيُعْدَمُ. وَالآنَ! اِغْرُبُوا عَنْ وَجْهي جَمِيعًا!" غَادَرَ الْجَمِيعُ الْمَكَانَ مُسْتَجِيبِينَ لِأَوَامِرِ أَمِيرِهِمِ الْغَاضِبِ.

في هَذِهِ الْأَثْنَاءِ كَانَتْ جُولْيِيتْ في غُرْفَتِها تَنْتَظِرُ غُرُوبَ الشَّمْسِ بِفَارِغِ الصَّبْرِ عَلَى أَمَلِ مُلَاقَاةِ زَوْجِها رُومْيُو وَاحْتِضَانِهِ. كَانَتْ تَعُدُّ الدَّقَائِقَ وَالثَّوَاني في ضَجَرٍ.

وَفَجْأَةً، دَخَلَتْ عَلَيْها مُرَبِّيَتُها حَامِلَةً سُلَّمًا. قَفَزَتْ جُولْيِيتْ مِنْ مَكَانِها وَسَأَلَتْها في حَمَاسٍ: "أَهَذا هُوَ السُّلَّمُ الَّذي طَلَبَهُ رُومْيُو؟"

"نَعَمْ" أَجَابَتْها الْمُرَبِّيَةُ في جَفَافٍ.

"حَسَنًا وَهَلْ مِنْ أَخْبارٍ جَدِيدَةٍ؟"

تَنَهَّدَتِ الْمُرَبِّيَةُ وَقَالَتْ في أَسَى: "إِنَّهُ لَيَوْمٌ حَزِينٌ كَئِيبٌ! لَقَدْ مَاتَ! لَقَدْ مَاتَ! يَا لَهُ مِنْ يَوْمٍ! لَقَدْ قُتِلَ! لَقَدْ قُتِلَ! قَتَلُوهُ..."

ظَنَّتْ جُولْيِيتْ أَنَّ الْمُرَبِّيَةَ كَانَتْ تَقْصِدُ رُومْيُو فَكَادَتْ تُصْعَقُ مِنْ قَسْوَةِ الْخَبَرِ وَانْهَارَتْ. إِلَّا أَنَّ الْمُرَبِّيَةَ سُرْعَانَ ما أَوْضَحَتْ قَصْدَها

قائِلَةً: "رومْيو قَتَلَ تَيْبالْتْ وَنُفِيَ مِنْ مَدينَةِ فيرونا... إِلَى الْأَبَدِ! رومْيو! رومْيو قَتَلَ تَيْبالْتْ..."

"أَيُّ نَوْعٍ مِنَ الرِّجالِ هُوَ زَوْجي؟ إِنَّني لا أُصَدِّقُ! أَهُوَ طاغِيَةٌ وَسيمٌ أَمْ مَلاكٌ شَيْطانِيٌّ؟ أَهُوَ وَحْشٌ مُتَنَكِّرٌ في شَكْلِ وَرْدَةٍ رَقيقَةٍ؟ أَمْ هُوَ غُرابٌ مَكْسُوٌّ بِريشِ الْيَمامِ؟ لِمَ جَسَدُهُ الْجَميلُ يَحْمِلُ روحًا شِرِّيرَةً هَكَذا؟ لِمَ؟ إِنَّني لا أُصَدِّقُ هَذا الْخَبَرَ...رومْيو قَتَلَ تَيْبالْتْ..." قالَتْ جوليِيتْ في حَيْرَةٍ.

"هَكَذا هُمْ كُلُّ الرِّجالِ" رَدَّتِ الْمُرَبِّيَةُ "لَيْسوا مَحَلَّ ثِقَةٍ وَلا يُمْكِنُ تَصْديقُهُمْ في شَيْءٍ... كُلُّهُمْ يَكْذِبونَ... اللَّعْنَةُ عَلَيْكَ يا رومْيو!"

فاسْتَشاطَتْ جولييتْ غَضَبًا عَلَى مُرَبِّيَتِها وَصَرَخَتْ في وَجْهِها: "إِيّاكِ أَنْ تُكَرِّريها! أَهَذا مَفْهومٌ؟ كَيْفَ اسْتَطَعْتُ أَنْ أَغْضَبَ مِنْ زَوْجي الْعَزيزِ؟ يَجِبُ أَنْ أَفْرَحَ لِأَنَّهُ عَلَى قَيْدِ الْحَياةِ!"

"أَتُدافِعينَ عَنْ مَنْ قَتَلَ ابْنَ عَمِّكِ؟ هَلْ جُنِنْتِ أَمْ ماذا؟" سَأَلَتْها الْمُرَبِّيَةُ.

"وَهَلْ تُريدينَ أَنْ أَقِفَ ضِدَّ زَوْجي؟ وَماذا لَوْ قَتَلَ تَيْبالْتْ رومْيو؟ ماذا

سَيَكونُ مَصيري جينها؟ عَلَيَّ أَنْ أَسْعَدَ لِأَنَّ زَوْجي بِخَيْرٍ وَلَمْ يُصِبْهُ مَكروهٌ... إِلَّا أَنَّهُ... قَدْ... نُفيَ مِنَ الْمَدينَةِ... وَهَذا الْخَبَرُ أَبْشَعُ وَأَقْسَى مِنْ خَبَرِ مَقْتَلِ الآلافِ مِنْ تَيْبالْتَ... زَوْجي الْحَبيبُ قَدْ نُفيَ! لا توجَدُ كَلِماتٌ تَصِفُ آلامي وَتُعَبِّرُ عَنْ مَأْساتي..." وانهارَتْ جوليِيتْ باكِيَةً.

في هَذِهِ اللَّحَظاتِ، كانَ السَّيِّدُ كابوليتْ وَزَوْجَتُهُ يَبْكِيانِ جُثَّةَ تَيْبالْتْ، أَمَّا ابْنَتُهُما فَكانَ كُلُّ هَمِّها روميو وَقَرارُ إِقْصائِهِ مِنَ الْمَدينَةِ.

فَرَأَفَتِ الْمُرَبِّيَةُ بِحالِها وَوَعَدَتْها أَنْ تُحْضِرَ لَها زَوْجَها في اللَّيلِ، فَهِيَ تَعْرِفُ جَيِّدًا أَيْنَ يَخْتَبِئُ: "لا تَقْلَقي آنِسَتي... سَتَلْتَقينَ بِهِ اللَّيْلَةَ، فَلا تَحْزَني أَرْجوكِ!"

مَسَحَتْ جوليِيتْ دُموعَها وَنَزَعَتْ خاتَمًا مِنْ إِصْبَعِها وَقَدَّمَتْهُ لِمُرَبِّيَتِها قائِلَةً: "شُكْرًا لَكِ مُرَبِّيَتي... خُذي هَذا الْخاتَمَ واعْطيهِ لِزَوْجي وَأَخْبِريهِ بِأَنَّني أَنْتَظِرُهُ... لِكَيْ أُوَدِّعَهُ الْوَداعَ الْأَخيرَ..." أَخَذَتِ الْمُرَبِّيَةُ الْخاتَمَ وانْصَرَفَتْ.

# Vocabulary

### p. 79

حَرارَةٌ heat
تَجَوُّلٌ wandering, going out
طَقْسٌ (طُقوسٌ) weather
مالَ إلى (مَيْلٌ) [1h2] to have a propensity for, tend toward

عُنْفٌ violence
سُخْرِيَّةٌ sarcasm, mockery
طَبْعٌ (طِباعٌ) nature, disposition

### p. 80

غابَ (غِيابٌ) [1h2] to be absent
اِخْتِلاقٌ fabricating, fabrication
اِفْتَعَلَ (اِفْتِعالٌ) [2s] to invent
تَسَكَّعَ (تَسَكُّعٌ) [5s] to hang out
بِتْروكيو Petruchio (name)
تَوَجَّهَ بِـ إلى [2s] to turn toward
مُتَوَخِّيًا الحَذَرَ cautiously
اِنْتَقى [8d1] to choose, pick
خالَ (خَيْلٌ) [1h1] to consider, deem

مُتَجَوِّلٌ roaming, wandering, touring
وَتَرٌ (أوْتارٌ) (instrument) string
اِسْتِهْزاءٌ mockery
رَصانَةٌ poise, solemnity
عَقْلانِيَّةٌ rationality
غُرورٌ arrogance
خُلِقَ (خَلْقٌ) [1s3] pass. to be created
نَظَرٌ (أنْظارٌ) sight, gaze; attention

### p. 81

مَعْنيٌّ meaning
حِقْدٌ (أحْقادٌ) hatred
نَذْلٌ (أنْذالٌ) coward, scoundrel
غَفَرَ (مَغْفِرَةٌ/غُفْرانٌ) [1s2] to forgive
شَتيمَةٌ (شَتائِمُ) insult

أصْلَحَ [4s] to repair, mend
مُخْطِئٌ wrong
عَلى العَكْسِ on the contrary
صُدِمَ بِـ (صَدْمٌ) [1s2] pass. to be shocked by

عارٌ (أَعْيَارٌ) shame
قَبِلَ (قَبُولٌ) [1s4] to accept

صَدٌّ (صُدُودٌ) prevention

## p. 82

ذِرَاعٌ (أَذْرُعٌ) arm
إِصَابَةٌ injury, affliction
خَطِيرٌ (خُطُرٌ) serious, grave
أَوْقَعَ بِـ [4a2] to bring down, assault
أَرْضٌ (أَرَاضٍ) ground, land
تَخَبَّطَ [5s] to roll, wallow
فَرَّ (فِرَارٌ) [1g2] to flee, escape
جَرَى (جَرْيٌ) [1d2] to run
فَتَّشَ عَنْ [2s] to search for
مُصَابٌ injured
كَفَّ عَنْ (كَفٌّ) [1g3] to stop, quit, abstain from
سَبَّ (سَبٌّ) [1g3] to insult
شَتَمَ (شَتْمٌ) [1s3] to insult
اللَّتَانِ dual who, which, that

تَأَلَّمَ [5s(a)] to suffer
أُحْتُضِرَ [8s1] pass. to die
مَاكِثٌ staying
تَأْثِيرٌ effect
صَدْمَةٌ shock
دِفَاعٌ عَنْ defense of
حِمَايَةٌ protecting, protection
مُذْنِبٌ guilty; culprit
وَفَاةٌ (وَفَيَاتٌ) death, passing away
عَلَّقَ عَلَى [3s] to comment on
مُرِيعٌ terrible, terrifying, horrible
مُقْبِلٌ future, coming
بَشَاعَةٌ wickedness, ugliness

## p. 83

آنَ الأَوَانُ لِـ it is high time that...
ثَأَرَ لِـ (ثَأْرٌ) [1s1(a)] to avenge
رُوحٌ (أَرْوَاحٌ) soul, spirit
طَافَ (طَوْفٌ) [1h3] to wander about, roam
مُلَاقَاةٌ meeting
إِمَّا... أَوْ... either... or...
كِلَانَا both of us
اِسْتَخَفَّ بِـ [10g] to look down on
بِعُنْفٍ violently

تَخَاصَمَ [6s] to fight, quarrel
سَقَطَ مَغْشِيًّا عَلَيْهِ (سُقُوطٌ) [1s3] to pass out, lose consciousness
لَفَظَ (لَفْظٌ) [1s2] to expel
مَارٌّ (مَارَّةٌ) pedestrian, passer-by
جُثَّةٌ (جُثَثٌ) corpse, dead body
حَكَمَ عَلَى (حُكْمٌ) [1s3] to sentence, impose upon
إِعْدَامٌ execution, death penalty
مَوْقِعٌ (مَوَاقِعُ) location, place

| | |
|---|---|
| (حُصولٌ) حَصَلَ [1s3] to happen, occur | شارَكَ في [3s] to participate in<br>مَوْلايَ your majesty |

*p. 84*

| | |
|---|---|
| مُتَجاهِلٌ ignorant | مَقْتولٌ dead, killed |
| (قَتْلى) قَتيلٌ dead, killed | تَشاجَرَ مَعَ [6a] to fight, quarrel with |
| ثَأْرٌ vengeance, revenge | انْهارَ [7h] to collapse |
| مُتَوَحِّشٌ savage | لَدى رُؤْيَةِ at the sight of |
| (اتِّخاذٌ) اتَّخَذَ [8a1] to adopt, take | حَيْرَةٌ confusion |
| عادِلٌ fair | بَراءَةٌ innocence |
| حاسِمٌ decisive | (ظَلَمَةٌ) ظالِمٌ in the wrong, unjust |
| مِنَ الْيَوْمِ فَصاعِدًا from now on | (دُعاءٌ) دَعا [1d3] to invite, ask; to pray |
| مُقْصًى مِنْ expelled, exiled | |
| (حُتوفٌ) حَتْفٌ death, demise | |

*p. 85*

| | |
|---|---|
| (قَفْزٌ) قَفَزَ [1s2] to jump | أُعْدِمَ [4s] *pass.* to be executed, put to death |
| (قَتْلٌ) قُتِلَ [1s3] *pass.* to be killed | (غَرْبٌ) غَرَبَ [1s3] to go away |
| (صاعِقَةٌ) صُعِقَ [1s1] *pass.* to be amazed, stunned | (احْتِضانٌ) احْتَضَنَ [8s1] to embrace, hug |
| أَوْضَحَ [4a1] to explain, clarify | ضَجَرٌ boredom |

*p. 86*

| | |
|---|---|
| ثِقَةٌ confidence, trust | (نَفْيٌ) نُفِيَ [1d2] to be banished |
| لَعْنَةٌ curse | (آبادٌ) أَبَدٌ eternity |
| كَرَّرَ [2s] to repeat, do again | (طُغاةٌ) طاغِيَةٌ tyrant |
| (غَضَبٌ) غَضِبَ مِنْ [1s4] to be angry at | شَيْطانِيٌّ demonic, devilish |
| (فَرَحٌ) فَرِحَ [1s4] to be happy, overjoyed | مَكْسُوٌّ بِـ covered, clothed in |
| دافَعَ عَنْ [3s] to defend | ريشٌ *coll.* feathers |
| | شِرِّيرٌ evil |
| | مَحَلٌّ object (of) |

| | |
|---|---|
| وَقَفَ (وُقوفٌ/وَقُفٌ) [1a2] to stand | جُنَّ (جُنونٌ) [1g3] to go crazy |

*p. 87*

| | |
|---|---|
| اِخْتَبَأ [8s(c)] to hide | حينَها then |
| مَسَحَ (مَسْحٌ) [1s1] to wipe | أَبْشَعُ ugly; *elative* |
| خاتَمٌ (خَواتِمُ) ring | وَصَفَ (وَصْفَةٌ) [1a2] to describe |
| قَدَّمَ [2s] to offer | أَلَمٌ (آلامٌ) pain |
| وَداعٌ farewell | مَأْساةٌ (مَآسٍ) tragedy, drama |
| اِنْصَرَفَ run along | إِقْصاءٌ removal, elimination |
| | رَأَفَ بِ (رَأْفَةٌ) [1s1(a)] to show mercy on, pity |

## Translation

*p. 79*

The weather was very hot and Mercutio was trying to persuade Benvolio to go out, but the latter had no desire to do so.

"Mercutio, please! I do not want to go out now. The weather is hot and I wouldn't want to fight with any of the Capulets... for as you know, heat makes us lose our temper quickly and tend to fight and to be violent!"

Mercutio answered him sarcastically, "You speak as if the heat is really the cause of your violence, but in fact, you are violent by nature! You are always on edge...

*p. 80*

Even when all reasons for fighting are absent, you are able to fabricate and make things so they'll fight!" Mercutio continued provoking Benvolio, trying to persuade him to hang out around the city a little, until they saw Tybalt approaching them with Petruchio and other members of the Capulet family.

"I want to talk to one of you, please," Tybalt said, addressing Mercutio and Benvolio while Petruchio cautiously stood close to him. He continued, "Mercutio, you are very close to Romeo and you often hang out together..." Mercutio interrupted him in anger, "What did you say? Hanging out together? Don't you know how to choose your words? Are we musicians in a band or what? If you think so, I will play you great music and make you dance on its strings!" He pointed to his weapon in mockery.

Benvolio was troubled and tried to calm the atmosphere, "We are in a public place, guys, so calm down, please, and speak wisely and rationally, or go somewhere else, away from people's eyes."

Mercutio replied arrogantly, "People's eyes were created to see, so let everyone see! I will not move from here."

*p. 81*

Then Romeo joined them. Tybalt looked at him, addressing Mercutio, "You're done here. The real [fight] has arrived, Romeo!" Tybalt shouted in hatred, "You bastard!"

Romeo replied calmly, "Tybalt! Do you know that there is something that makes me love you and forget about the hatred between us and forgive you your insults? I'm not a scoundrel, Tybalt... Goodbye!"

"Your words will not convince me, nor will they mend what you've done, so come back right now and let's fight."

Romeo answered, "You're wrong, Tybalt! I did not do anything to you. On the contrary, I love you more than you could imagine. You will find out later why, so you have to be happy with this."

Mercutio was shocked by Romeo's answer and said in amazement, "What you have just said, Romeo, is shameful to you and to all of us! I will end this matter immediately!" And he drew his sword in the face of Tybalt, who accepted the challenge.

Despite Romeo's attempts to prevent them from fighting, threatening them with the prince's presence,

*p. 82*

they ignored him. As they fought, Romeo stood between them. Tybalt stabbed Mercutio from under Romeo's arm and hit him so hard that it caused him to fall down bleeding.

Tybalt and his men escaped, while Mercutio's servant went searching for a doctor for his master. Benvolio carried his injured friend to a nearby house in the hope of saving him while Mercutio kept insulting the Montagues and the Capulets, because of whom he was suffering... and perhaps dying!

Romeo stood in place, thinking in shock, "My poor friend Mercutio! He will lose his life because of me. He was trying to defend me and protect me from Tybalt. I am the culprit... I am the culprit..."

Benvolio interrupted him, announcing the news of the death of their friend and kinsman of the Prince of Verona, Mercutio! Romeo commented on the news in pain, "This is terrible news and the beginning of the bloody events that we will witness in the coming days... and which will end with horror!"

As soon as he finished his words, Tybalt had returned to him. Romeo looked at him...

*p. 83*

in hatred and said to him, "It is high time I took revenge for myself and for Mercutio, whose spirit is still hovering around us and waiting to meet your spirit! Let's fight, Tybalt! And one of us will join Mercutio today! Either I, you, or both of us!"

Tybalt rushed towards Romeo, looking at him in disdain, and began to fight violently. They fought with their weapons until Tybalt fell to the ground, unconscious, expelling his last breaths, under the sight of pedestrians who gathered to watch what was going on.

Romeo stood looking at the body of Tybalt in astonishment. Benvolio shouted out, "Romeo get out of here! People have witnessed the fight, and the prince will sentence you to death! Please, get out of here!"

༄ ༄ ༄

The Prince arrived at the scene of the fight, accompanied by Lord Montague and his wife, Lord Capulet and his wife, and other men. The Prince shouted, "Bring me all those who participated in this bloody scene!"

Benvolio pulled himself together and said, "Your Highness! I can tell you what happened!...

*p. 84*

Here is Tybalt dead. He killed one of your loyal relatives! It's Mercutio! He fled and then he came back to Romeo and fought with him. The latter killed him."

Lady Capulet collapsed when she saw the body of Tybalt and begged the Prince to avenge her and kill a member of the Montague family.

While the prince was confused, Benvolio tried to defend Romeo and convince the Prince of his innocence, and went on to say, "Tybalt, your Highness, is at fault and the one who started the fight. Romeo asked him to calm down, in vain. Tybalt quarreled with Mercutio, ignoring Romeo's advice until he was killed. Then he came back to provoke Romeo, who was sad over the death of his friend, again. And then... he took revenge on the savage Tybalt and killed him. This is all true, your highness!"

The prince, who was trying to make a fair decision on both sides, became more perplexed, while the Capulets tried to defend their son Tybalt, and the Montague family was trying to save Romeo's fate. After a long hesitation, the prince announced his final decision, "From now on... Romeo is exiled from Verona. He will never return to it! My kinsman, Mercutio, died...

*p. 85*

because of your hatred. Romeo must immediately leave the city, or else he will be put to death. And now, get out of my face!" Everyone left the place, obeying the orders of their angry prince.

ೲ ೲ ೲ

In the meantime, Juliet was in her room waiting for the sun to set, hoping to meet her husband, Romeo, and embrace him. She was counting minutes and seconds in boredom.

Suddenly, her nanny entered carrying a ladder. Juliet jumped out of her seat and asked her excitedly, "Is this the ladder that Romeo asked for?"

"Yes," the nanny answered firmly.

"Well, is there any news?"

The nanny sighed and said in sorrow, "It is a very sad day! He's dead! He's dead! What a day! He was killed! He was killed! They killed him."

Juliet thought that the nanny was talking about Romeo. She was shocked by the harshness of the news and collapsed. But the nanny quickly explained,...

*p. 86*

"Romeo killed Tybalt and was exiled from the city of Verona... forever! Romeo! Romeo killed Tybalt..."

"What kind of man is my husband? I cannot believe it! Is he a handsome tyrant or a fiendish angel? Is he a disguised monster in the shape of a tender rose? Or is he a raven with the feathers of a dove? Why does his beautiful body possess such an evil spirit? Why? I do not believe this... Romeo killed Tybalt..." Juliet said in confusion.

"So are all men,"The nanny replied. "They are not trustworthy and cannot be believed in anything. They are all liars. Damn you, Romeo!"

Juliet was furious at her nanny and yelled at her, "Do not say that again! Is this understood? How could I be angry with my dear husband? I should be happy because he is alive!"

"Do you defend the one who killed your cousin? Are you crazy or what?" the nanny asked her.

"Do you want me to stand against my husband? And what if Romeo was killed by Tybalt? What...

*p. 87*

would be my fate then? I have to be happy because my husband is fine and did not get hurt... but he... has... been exiled from the city. This news is uglier and worse than the murder of ten thousand Tybalts. My beloved husband has been banished! There are no words that could describe my pain and express my sorrow." Juliet collapsed crying.

At that same moment, Lord Capulet and his wife were weeping over the body of Tybalt, while their daughter was only worried about Romeo and the decision of his banishment from the city. The nanny felt sorry for her and promised to bring her husband at night, for she knew very well where he was hiding.

"Do not worry, my lady... You will meet him tonight. Do not be sad, please!"

Juliet wiped her tears and removed a ring from her finger and offered it to her nanny, saying, "Thank you, nanny. Take this ring and give it to my husband and tell him that I am waiting for him... to give him a final farewell."

The nanny took the ring and left.

# اَلْفَصْلُ السَّادِسُ

أَخْبَرَ الْقِسِّيسُ لورِنْس روميو بِقَرارِ الْأَميرِ وَالَّذي كانَ يَقْتَضي إِقْصاءَهُ نِهائِيًّا مِنْ مَدينَةِ فيرونا.

"إِنَّ الْمَوْتَ أَرْفَقُ مِنْ هذا الْقَرارِ! أَرْجوكَ يا أَبَتِ قُلْ لي أَنَّهُ حَكَمَ عَلَيَّ بِالْإِعْدامِ! أَرْجوكَ! فَخارِجَ أَسْوارِ مَدينَةِ فيرونا لا توجَدُ حَياةٌ... لا يوجَدُ شَيْءٌ سِوى الْجَحيمِ وَالْعَذابِ... وَانَّ إِقْصائي مِنْ فيرونا يَعْني إِقْصائي مِنَ الْعالَمِ... وَإِقْصائي مِنَ الْعالَمِ يَعْني الْمَوْتُ! أَتَفْهَمُ مَدى قَسْوَةِ هذا الْقَرارِ؟ إِنَّهُ أَبْشَعُ مِنَ الْمَوْتِ نَفْسِهِ..." عَلَّقَ روميو في يَأْسٍ.

فَأَجابَهُ الرَّاهِبُ لورنس في عِتابٍ: "يا لَكَ مِنْ ناكِرٍ لِلْجَميلِ! إنَّ ما أَقْدَمْتَ عَلَى فِعْلِهِ يَسْتَحِقُّ عُقوبَةَ الإعدامِ... أتفْهَمْ؟ عُقوبَةَ الإعدامِ يا روميو! إلّا أنَّ أميرَنا قَدْ أشْفَقَ عَلَيْكَ واِكْتَفَى بِنَفْيِكَ مِنَ الْمَدينَةِ. عَلَيْكَ أَنْ تَكونَ مُمْتَنًّا لَهُ يا بُنَيَّ..."

غَرِقَ روميو في أفْكارِهِ الْبَشِعَةِ سائلًا نَفْسَهُ: "كَيْفَ سَأفْعَلُ الآنَ بَعيدًا عَنْ حَبيبَتي؟ بَعيدًا عَنْ زَوْجَتي؟ ما هُوَ مَصيري؟ ما مَصيرُها؟ ما مَصيرُنا يا تُرى؟ كَيْفَ سَأعيشُ بِدونِها وَبَعيدًا عَنْها؟ وَهَلْ سَتَقْدِرُ هِيَ عَلَى الْعَيْشِ بِدوني؟ سَأشْتاقُ إلَيْها... إلى وَجْهِها... إلى شَفَتَيْها... إلى جَمالِها... إلى رِقَّتِها... آهٍ! سَأشْتاقُ إلى زَوْجَتي الْحَبيبَةِ... الْمَوْتُ أهْوَنُ بِكَثيرٍ مِنَ الْعَيْشِ بِدونِ جولييت!"

كانَ الْقِسّيسُ يُحاوِلُ مُواساتَهُ إلّا أنَّ روميو كانَ يَتَخَبَّطُ حُزْنًا. وَفَجْأةً، طُرِقَ بابُ الْخَلْوَةِ فالْتَفَتَ لورنس إلى روميو في فَزَعٍ، وَهَمَسَ إلَيْهِ مُحَذِّرًا: "إنْتَبِهْ روميو وَانْهَضْ وَاخْتَبِئْ حالًا، أظُنُّ أنَّهُمْ أتَوْا لِأخْذِكَ خارِجَ الْمَدينَةِ! هَيّا اذْهَبْ!"

فَتَحَ لورنس بابَهُ لِيَجِدَ مُرَبِّيَةَ جولييت أمامَهُ وَقَدْ كادَ صَبْرُها يَنْفَذُ مِنْ طولِ انْتِظارِها. وَبِدونِ اسْتِئْذانٍ، دَخَلَتْ وَأغْلَقَتِ الْبابَ وَرائَها.

"أَيْنَ هوَ؟ أَيْنَ هُوَ زَوْجُ آنِسَتي يا أَبَتِ؟" سَأَلَتِ الْمُرَبِّيَةُ الْكاهِنَ في تَوَتُّرٍ.

"ها هُوَ غارِقٌ في دُموعِهِ..." أَجابَها لورِنْسُ مُشيرًا إِلى روميو.

تَنَهَّدَتِ الْمُرَبِّيَةُ وَقالَتْ في أَسَفٍ: "اَلْمِسْكينُ، حالُهُ كَحالِ آنِسَتي..." واقْتَرَبَتْ مِنْهُ لِتواسيهِ.

رَفَعَ روميو رَأْسَهُ، فَفوجِئَ بِرُؤْيَةِ الْمُرَبِّيَةِ، وَعادَ إِلَيْهِ الْقَليلُ مِنَ الْأَمَلِ مُجَدَّدًا فَسَأَلَها: "أَرْجوكِ أَخْبِريني أَيْنَ هِيَ حَبيبَتي؟ وَكَيْفَ حالُها؟ هَلْ تَظُنُّني مُجْرِمٌ قاتِلٌ؟ قولي لِيَ الْحَقيقَةَ أَرْجوكِ..."

"لا تَقْلَقْ يا سَيِّدي فَهِيَ مُنْهارَةٌ بِسَبَبِ قَرارِ نَفْيِكَ مِنَ الْمَدينَةِ، وَتَبْكيكَ بِحُرْقَةٍ... كَما أَنَّها مُشْتاقَةٌ إِلَيْكَ جِدًّا..."

وَلَمْ تَكَدِ الْمُرَبِّيَةُ تُنْهي كَلامَها حَتَّى سَلَّ روميو سَيْفَهُ وَكَأَنَّهُ يَهُمُّ بِقَتْلِ نَفْسِهِ.

فَصاحَ لورِنْسُ في غَضَبٍ: "ما الَّذي تَفْعَلُهُ؟ هَلْ جُنِنْتَ؟ اهْدَأْ حالًا وَكُنْ رَجُلًا! إِنَّ مَظْهَرَكَ مَظْهَرُ رَجُلٍ إِلَّا أَنَّ تَصَرُّفاتِكَ تَصَرُّفاتُ امْرَأَةٍ... ضَعيفَةٍ... مَهْزومَةٍ! ما كُلُّ هَذا الْإِنْفِعالِ؟ أَلا تَخْجَلُ مِنْ

نَفْسِكَ؟ كُنْتُ أَظُنُّكَ ذَكِيًّا وَفَطِنًا... وَلَكِنَّكَ خَيَّبْتَ آمالي. أَهذا كُلُّ ما تَسْتَطيعُ فِعْلَهُ؟ قَتْلُ نَفْسِكَ؟ يا لَكَ مِنْ جَبانٍ! أَلَمْ تُفَكِّرْ وَلَوْ لِلَحْظَةٍ بِمَصيرِ زَوْجَتِكَ إِنْ قَتَلْتَ نَفْسَكَ؟ أَهذا هُوَ الْحُبُّ الَّذي وَعَدْتَهُ لَها وَوَعَدْتُها أَنْ تُحافِظَ عَلَيْهِ؟ كَلامُكَ كَذِبٌ وَهُراءٌ... أَنْتَ الآنَ بِصَدَدِ قَتْلِ ذَلِكَ الْحُبِّ الَّذي مِنَ الْمُفْتَرَضِ أَنْ تَصونَهُ! هَيّا انْهَضْ! وَكُنْ رَجُلًا! اِنْهَضْ وَاسْعَدْ لِأَنَّ حَبيبَتَكَ بِخَيْرٍ وَعَلَى قَيْدِ الْحَياةِ، وَلِأَنَّكَ أَيْضًا بِخَيْرٍ وَعَلَى قَيْدِ الْحَياةِ... افْرَحْ لِأَنَّ الْحَياةَ مُسْتَمِرَّةٌ، وَلِأَنَّ الْقَدَرَ غَيَّرَ عُقوبَتَكَ مِنَ الْإِعْدامِ إِلَى النَّفْيِ... أُبَشِّرُ بِحَياةٍ جَديدَةٍ وُهِبَتْ إِلَيْكَ، وَبِحَبيبَةٍ وَفِيَّةٍ تَنْتَظِرُكَ بِفارِغِ الصَّبْرِ... وَاسْتَمْتِعْ بِحَياةٍ جَميلَةٍ مَليئَةٍ بِالنِّعَمِ! هَيّا انْهَضْ وَالتَحِقْ بِحَبيبَتِكَ فَهِيَ مُحْتاجَةٌ إِلَيْكَ... اِذْهَبْ قَبْلَ سُقوطِ اللَّيْلِ وَانْتِشارِ الْجُرْذانِ! ثُمَّ عَلَيْكَ أَنْ تَهْرُبَ إِلَى مَدينَةِ مَنْتُوا أَيْنَ سَتَمْكُثُ حَتَّى نُعْلِنَ خَبَرَ زَواجِكُما وَتَتَصالَحَ الْعائِلَتانِ وَتَعودَ أَنْتَ إِلَى فيرونا بَيْنَنا." وَالْتَفَتَ لورِنْسُ إِلَى الْمُرَبِّيَةِ قائِلًا: "وَأَنْتِ أَيَّتُها الْمُرَبِّيَةُ، بَلِّغي سَلامي إِلَى آنِسَتِكِ الفاضِلَةِ، وَأَخْبِريها أَنَّ زَوْجَها سَيَزورُها اللَّيْلَةَ!"

"يا لَهُ مِنْ كَلامٍ رائِعٍ يا أَبَتِ! وَيا لَها مِنْ نَصائِحَ ثَمينَةٍ! حَسَنًا سَأَذْهَبُ وَأُخْبِرُها" أَجابَتْهُ الْمُرَبِّيَةُ. وَقَبْلَ أَنْ تَنْصَرِفَ، مَدَّتْ بِالْخاتِمِ

إلى رومْيو فَشَكَرَها هذا الأخيرُ وَتَنَفَّسَ الصُّعَداء.

نَظَرَ القِسِّيسُ إلى رومْيو وقالَ لَهُ: "هَيَّا أَسْرِعْ يا بُنَيَّ، وَأَنا سَأُوافِيكَ بِكُلِّ الأخبارِ عَنْ طَريقِ رَسولٍ! اِتَّفَقْنا؟"

"اتَّفَقْنا" أجابَهُ رومْيو في اِمْتِنانٍ.

"وَداعًا"

"وَداعًا"

في هَذِهِ الأَثْناءِ كانَ السَّيِّدُ كابوليت مُجْتَمِعًا بِزَوْجَتِهِ وبِالسَّيِّدِ باريس. قَدَّمَ السَّيِّدُ كابوليت اِعْتِذاراتِهِ إلى باريسْ قائِلًا: "أَعْتَذِرُ لَكَ يا ابني، لَمْ أَجِدِ الوَقْتَ لِأُقْنِعَ جولييت بِالزَّواجِ مِنْكَ، فَكَما تَعْلَمُ، اِبْنَتي لا تَزالُ حَزينةً عَلى مَوْتِ تَيْبالْتْ اِبْنَ عَمِّها..." والتَفَتَ إلى زَوْجَتِهِ مُضيفًا: "تَحَدَّثي مَعَ ابْنَتِكِ واقنِعيها بِالزَّواجِ مِنْ باريسْ! سَيَكونُ الزِّفافُ يَوْمَ الخَميسِ. وقولي لَها أَلّا تَقْلَقَ، فَلَنْ نُقيمَ حَفْلًا هائِلًا، سَيَكونُ حَفْلًا بَسيطًا يَشْمَلُ الأقارِبَ فَقَط، فَنَحْنُ لا نَزالُ في حِدادٍ عَلى عَزيزِنا تَيْبالْتْ..."

بَدا باريسُ مُتَفَهِّمًا وَكادَ يَطيرُ فَرَحًا، فَشَكَرَ والِدَ جولييت وانصَرَفَ يَحْلُمُ بِيَوْمِ الْخَميسِ.

أمَّا روميو، فَتَسَلَّلَ كَالْعادَةِ إلى شُرْفَةِ جولييت أيْنَ مَكَثا يَتَحَدَّثانِ لِساعاتٍ وَساعاتٍ حَتّى اخْتَلَطَ اللَّيْلُ بِالنَّهارِ في ذِهْنِ روميو. لَقَدْ كانَ الْمِسْكينُ خائِفًا مِنْ طُلوعِ النَّهارِ، إلّا أنَّ جولييت طَمْأَنَتْهُ قائِلَةً: "لا تَقْلَقْ حَبيبي، فَالْوَقْتُ لا يَزالُ لَيْلًا. لا تَسْتَعْجِلْ أرْجوكَ... لا تَذْهَبْ!" أجابَها روميو: "حَسَنًا، حَسَنًا، لَنْ أذْهَبَ! إنْ كُنْتِ تُريدينَ مَوْتي فَلَكِ ذَلِكَ سَيِّدَتي!"

وَظَلّا هَكَذا يَتَجادَلانِ طِوالَ اللَّيْلَةِ حَتّى طُلوعِ الفَجْرِ. قَطَعَتْ حَديثَهُما الْمُرَبِّيَةُ مُحَذِّرَةً: "آنِسَتي! آنِسَتي! انْتَبِهي! والِدَتُكِ قادِمَةٌ إلى غُرْفَتِكِ! لَقَدْ طَلَعَ النَّهارُ!"

دَقَّتْ لَحْظَةُ الْوَداعِ، فَنَهَضَ روميو وجولييت وَعانَقا بَعْضَهُما الْبَعْضَ في حُزْنٍ ثُمَّ نَزَلَ روميو مُسْرِعًا وَغابَ عَنْ أنْظارِ زَوْجَتِهِ... عَلى أمَلِ لِقاءٍ قَريبٍ.

دَخَلَتِ السَّيِّدَةُ كابوليت غُرْفَةَ ابْنَتِها.

"كَيْفَ حالُكِ بُنَيَّتي؟ أَخْبِريني."

"أَحْوالي سَيِّئَةٌ لِلْغايَةِ يا أُمِّي" أَجابَتْها جولييت.

"هَلْ سَتَبْقَيْنَ هَكَذا طِيلَةَ حَياتَكِ تَبْكِينَ تَيْبالْتْ؟ امْسَحي دُموعَكِ وَكَفاكِ حُزْنًا يا ابْنَتي، فَبُكاؤُكِ لَنْ يُرْجِعَ تَيْبالْتْ... إِنَّ الْمُصيبَةَ الْأَكْبَرَ هِيَ أَنَّ قاتِلَهُ لا يَزالُ عَلَى قَيْدِ الْحَياةِ!" تَظاهَرَتْ جولييت بِالْجَهْلِ وَسَأَلَتْها: "وَمَنْ يَكونُ قاتِلُهُ؟"

"إِنَّهُ روميو الْمُجْرِمُ! روميو!"

"روميو لَيْسَ بِالْمُجْرِمِ!" قالَتْ جولييت في نَفْسِها ثُمَّ أَجابَتْ والِدَتَها: "يا لَيْتَني أَقْدِرُ عَلَى الْأَخْذِ بِثَأْرِ تَيْبالْتْ بِنَفْسي..."

"لا تَقْلَقي! كُلُّنا سَنَنْتَقِمُ لَهُ! سَوْفَ أُرْسِلُ رَسولًا إِلَى مَدينَةِ مَنْتوا أَيْنَ سَيُسَمِّمُ روميو وَيَقْتُلُهُ، وَسَتَفْرَحينَ بِخَبَرِ مَوْتِهِ!" قالَتِ السَّيِّدَةُ كابوليت.

"لا، لَنْ أَفْرَحَ... لَنْ أَفْرَحَ...حَتَّى أَراهُ... حَتَّى أَراهُ... مَيِّتًا... مَيِّتًا... مِثْلَ قَلْبي عِنْدَما أَتَذَكَّرُ ابْنَ عَمِّي. أَرْجوكِ دَعيني أُخْلِطُ

الْمَخْلُوطِ بِنَفْسِي! وَهٰكَذا سَأَقْتُلُهُ بِنَفْسِي!"

وَافَقَتْ وَالِدَتُها، وَسُرْعانَ ما غَيَّرَتِ الْمَوْضُوعَ مُعْلِنَةً خَبَرَ زِفافِ جُولِييتْ: "حَسَنًا، حَسَنًا، وَلٰكِنِ إِلَيْكِ بِالْأَخْبارِ السَّعِيدَةِ الآنَ! يَوْمَ الْخَمِيسِ في الصَّباحِ... هُوَ يَوْمُ زِفافِكِ! سَتَتَزَوَّجِينَ باريس!" فوجِئَتْ جُولِييتْ بِالْخَبَرِ الصَّادِمِ "ماذا؟ باريس؟ لَنْ يُسعِدَني أَبَدًا هٰذا الرَّجُلُ! أُفَضِّلُ الزَّواجَ مِنْ رومْيو الْقاتِلِ! أَخْبِري والِدي أَنْ يَتْرُكَني أُقابِلَهُ قَبْلَ الزَّواجِ عَلَى الْأَقَلِّ، فَأَنا بِالْكادِ أَعْرِفُهُ..."

"ها هُوَ والِدُكِ قَدْ أَتَى أَخْبِرِيهِ بِنَفْسِكِ!" أَجابَتْها السَّيِّدَةُ كابوليتْ في غَضَبٍ.

دَخَلَ عَلَيْهِما السَّيِّدُ كابوليتْ وَتَتْبَعُهُ الْمُرَبِّيَةُ، وَجَلَسَ يواسي ابْنَتَهُ. ثُمَّ الْتَفَتَ إِلَى زَوْجَتِهِ سَأَلَها إِنْ كانَتْ قَدْ أَخْبَرَتْ جُولِييتْ بِأَمْرِ الزِّفافِ، فَأَخْبَرَتْهُ السَّيِّدَةُ كابوليتْ بِأَنَّ جُولِييتْ رافِضَةٌ لِلْمَوْضُوعِ تَمامًا.

خَرَجَ السَّيِّدُ كابوليتْ مِنْ هُدوئِهِ وَصَرَخَ بِوَجْهِ جُولِييتْ: "ماذا؟ لَسْتِ مُوافِقَةً؟ يا لَكِ مِنْ ناكِرَةٍ لِلْجَمِيلِ! مِنَ الْمُفْتَرَضِ أَنْ تَكونِي سَعِيدَةً بِهٰذا الْقِرانِ الْعَظِيمِ! وَمِنَ الْمُفْتَرَضِ أَنْ تَكونِي مَدِينَةً لي أَيَّتُها الْفَتاةُ الْمُدَلَّلَةُ! أَلا تَخْجَلِي مِنْ نَفْسِكِ؟ هَيّا اسْتَعِدِّي لِزَواجِكِ... يَوْمَ

الْخَمِيسِ سَتَذْهَبِينَ إِلَى كَنِيسَةِ الْقِدِّيسِ بِيتر بِمَحْضِ إِرَادَتِكِ، وَإِلَّا سَأُرْغِمُكِ عَلَى الذَّهَابِ... أَتَفْهَمِينَ؟ وَالْآنَ اغْرُبِي عَنْ وَجْهِي!"

أَجْهَشَتْ جولييت بِالْبُكَاءِ فِي حِينَ حَاوَلَتِ الْمُرَبِّيَةُ الدِّفَاعَ عَنْهَا وَإِقْنَاعَ وَالِدَيْهَا بِالْاِسْتِمَاعِ إِلَيْهَا، إِلَّا أَنَّ السَّيِّدَ كابوليت وَزَوْجَتُهُ رَفَضَا بِقَسْوَةٍ. وَقَبْلَ أَنْ يَخْرُجَا مِنْ غُرْفَةِ جولييت، قَالَ لَهَا وَالِدُهَا مُهَدِّدًا: "إِمَّا أَنْ تَمْتَثِلِي لِأَوَامِرِي أَوْ سَأَرْمِيكِ فِي الشَّارِعِ وَسَتَمُوتِينَ جُوعًا وَبَرْدًا وَفَقْرًا... اِخْتَارِي!"

وَذَهَبَ تَارِكًا جولييت تَبْكِي بِحُرْقَةٍ وَتَبِعَتْهُ السَّيِّدَةُ كابوليت.

اِرْتَمَتْ جولييت فِي أَحْضَانِ مُرَبِّيَتِهَا طَالِبَةً مِنْهَا الْمُسَاعَدَةَ، فَأَشْفَقَتْ عَلَيْهَا الْمُرَبِّيَةُ وَحَضَنَتْهَا قَائِلَةً: "مَا رَأْيُكِ لَوْ تَتَزَوَّجِي بِبَارِيس؟ فرومِيو بَعِيدٌ عَنْكِ وَبَارِيس شَابٌّ وَسِيمٌ أَنِيقٌ وَسَيَجْعَلُكِ سَعِيدَةً فِي حَيَاتِكِ..."

صَدَمَ كَلَامُ الْمُرَبِّيَةِ جولييت. شَعَرَتْ وَكَأَنَّ الْعَالَمَ كُلَّهُ ضِدَّهَا. فَاسْتَجْمَعَتْ قُوَاهَا وَقَالَتْ: "حَسَنًا، مَعَكِ حَقٌّ، سَأَذْهَبُ إِلَى الْقِسِّيسِ لورنس وَسَأَعْتَرِفُ لَهُ بِكُلِّ خَطَايَايَ... أَرْجُوكِ أَخْبِرِي وَالِدَتِي."

"حَسَنًا آنِسَتي" أجابَتْها الْمُرَبِّيَةُ في حَماسٍ وَنَهَضَتْ مُسْرِعَةً.

أمَّا جولييت، فَحَدَّثَتْ نَفْسَها قائِلَةً: "يا لها مِنْ شِرِّيرَةٍ! لَعَنَتْها الْمَلائِكَة! تُريدُني أَنْ أَخونَ زَوْجي... يا لَها مِنْ مُنافِقَةٍ! لَنْ أُخْبِرَها بِشَيْءٍ! سَأَذْهَبُ إلى الْكاهِنِ لورِنْسْ... لَعَلَّهُ يَجِدُ لي حَلًّا لِحَياتي الْبائِسَةِ وَإلَّا... وَإلَّا فَسَأُنْهيها بِنَفْسي..."

# Vocabulary

### p. 100

اِقْتَضَى [8d1] to require
نِهائِيًّا finally
جَحيمٌ hell

عَذابٌ (أَعْذِبةٌ) torment
يَأْسٌ (يُؤوسٌ) desperate

### p. 101

راهِبٌ (رُهْبانٌ) monk
مِنْ ناكِرٍ لِلْجَميلِ ungrateful
أَقْدَمَ عَلَى (إِقْدامٌ) [4s] to tackle, undertake, venture (to do)
فِعْلٌ (أَفْعالٌ) act, action
عُقوبةٌ punishment, penalty
اِكْتَفَى بِ [8h1] to settle for
مُمْتَنٌّ grateful
اِشْتاقَ إِلَى [8h1] to miss
أَهْوَنُ easy; *elative* أَهْوَنُ easier

واسَى (مُواساةٌ) [3d] to console, comfort
طُرِقَ (طَرْقٌ) [1s3] *pass.* to be knocked (on)
خُلْوةٌ cell
اِنْتَبَهَ [8s1] to watch out
نَهَضَ (نَهْضٌ) [1s1] to stand up, get up
طولٌ (أَطْوالٌ) length
اِسْتِئْذانٌ permission
أَغْلَقَ [4s] to close

### p. 102

غارِقٌ drowning
حالٌ (أَحْوالٌ) condition, state
رَفَعَ (رَفْعٌ) [1s1] to raise, lift
فوجِئَ [3s] *pass.* to be surprised
مُجْرِمٌ criminal
مُنْهارٌ devastated
نَفْيٌ evile, banishment; denial

بِحُرْقةٍ ardently
لَمْ يَكَدْ barely
قَتْلٌ (فُتولٌ) killing
مَظْهَرٌ (مَظاهِرُ) appearance, looking
تَصَرُّفٌ action, behavior
ضَعيفٌ (ضُعَفاءُ) weak

مَهْزُومٌ defeated
اِنْفِعَالٌ action

خَجِلَ مِنْ (خَجَلٌ) [1s4] to be ashamed of, embarrassed by

## p. 103

ذَكِيٌّ (أَذْكِيَاءُ) intelligent, smart
فَطِنٌ (فُطُنٌ) clever
خَيَّبَ [2s] to disappoint
وَعَدَ (وَعْدٌ) [1a2] to promise
حَافَظَ عَلَى [3s] to keep, maintain
هُرَاءٌ nonsense
بِصَدَدٍ about to, going to
صَانَ (صِيَانَةٌ) [1h3] to keep, maintain
مُسْتَمِرٌّ continuing, continuous, ongoing
أَبْشَرَ [4s] to rejoice
وُهِبَ (وَهْبٌ) [1a1] to be granted, given
وَفِيٌّ (أَوْفِيَاءُ) loyal
مَلِيءٌ بِ full of

نِعْمَةٌ (نِعَمٌ) blessing, grace
مُحْتَاجٌ إِلَى in need of
سُقُوطُ اللَّيْلِ nightfall
اِنْتِشَارٌ spreading, diffusion, circulation
حَارِسٌ (حُرَّاسٌ) guard, sentry
مَنْتُوا Mantua (city)
مَكَثَ (مُكُوثٌ/مَكْثٌ) [1s3] to reside, dwell
تَصَالَحَ [6s] to reconcile, make up
عَادَ (عَوْدَةٌ/عَوْدٌ) [1h3] to return
أَيَّتُهَا o...! (vocative)
بَلَّغَ [2s] to communicate, tell, convey
مَدَّ بِ إِلَى (مَدٌّ) [1g3] to hand to

## p. 104

وَافَى بِ [3d] to communicate, tell, convey
اِتَّفَقَ [8a1] to agree
اِمْتِنَانٌ gratitude
وَدَاعًا goodbye
اِعْتِذَارٌ apology
مُضِيفٌ adding

أَلَّا (لَا + أَنْ) that not, not to...
هَائِلٌ enormous
شَمِلَ (شَمَلٌ/شُمُولٌ) [1s4] to include
أَقَارِبُ pl. relatives
لَا يَزَالُ still (does)
حِدَادٌ mourning

## p. 105

| | |
|---|---|
| مُتَفَهِّم understanding, open-minded | تَحادَثَ [6s] to talk |
| اِخْتَلَطَ [8s1] to be mixed | طِوال throughout |
| طَلَعَ (طُلوعٌ) [1s3] to ascend, rise | دَقَّ (دَقٌّ) [1g3] to strike, hit |
| اِسْتَعْجَلَ [10s] to hurry, rush | نَهَضَ (نُهوضٌ/نَهْضٌ) [1s1] to get up |
| | عانَقَ [3s] to hug, embrace |

## p. 106

| | |
|---|---|
| سَيِّئٌ bad | قَدَرَ عَلَى (قَدَرٌ) [1s4] to be able to |
| طيلَةَ throughout | اِنْتَقَمَ لِ [8s1] to avenge |
| بُكاءٌ crying | سَمَّمَ [2s] to poison |
| مُصيبَةٌ calamity | مَيِّتٌ (أَمْواتٌ) dead |
| تَظاهَرَ بِ [6s] to pretend | أَخْلَطَ [4s] to mix |
| جَهْلٌ ignorance | |

## p. 107

| | |
|---|---|
| مَخْلوطٌ mixture | عَلَى الأَقَلّ at least |
| وافَقَ [3s] to agree | تَبِعَ (تَبَعٌ) [1s4] to follow |
| زِفافٌ wedding | مُدَلَّلٌ spoiled |
| صادِمٌ shocking | اِسْتَعَدَّ [10g] to get ready |
| قابَلَ [3s] to meet | |

## p. 108

| | |
|---|---|
| قِدّيسٌ saint | فَقْرٌ (فُقورٌ) poverty |
| بِمَحْضِ إِرادَتِهِ voluntarily, willingly | اِخْتارَ [8h1] to choose |
| وَإِلّا otherwise | طَلَبَ (طَلَبٌ) [1s3] to ask for, request |
| أَرْغَمَ عَلَى [4s] to force (to) | مُساعَدَةٌ help |
| أَجْهَشَ [4s] to break into tears | حَضَنَ (حِضْنٌ) [1s3] to embrace, hug |
| بِقَسْوَةٍ severely, harshly | أَنيقٌ classy, elegant |
| جوعٌ hunger, starvation | صَدَمَ (صَدْمٌ) [1s2] to shock |
| بَرْدٌ cold(ness) | |

خَطيئَةٌ (خَطايَا) sin

## p. 109

حَدَّثَ [2s] to speak to  
خانَ (خِيانَةٌ) [1h3] to betray  
مُنافِقَةٌ hypocrisy

شَيْءٌ (أَشْياءُ) thing; something  
حَلٌّ (حُلولٌ) solution  
بائِسٌ (بُؤَساءُ) miserable

# Translation

*p. 100*

Father Lawrence told Romeo about the prince's decision, which required his exile from Verona.

"Death is more merciful than this decision! Please, Father, tell me that I was sentenced to death! I beg you! For, outside the walls of the city of Verona, there is no life. There is nothing but hell and torment. My exclusion from Verona means exclusion from the world. And my exclusion from the world means death! Do you understand how harsh this decision is? It is even worse than death itself," Romeo said in despair.

*p. 101*

Father Lawrence replied to him, "Oh, how ungrateful you are! What you have committed deserves the death penalty. Do you understand? The death penalty, Romeo! But our prince has had mercy on you, and he has just banished you from the city. You have to be grateful to him, my son."

Romeo drowned in his hideous thoughts asking himself, "How will I go on without my love? Without my wife? What will be my fate? And what about hers? What about our fate? How will I live without her and away from her? Will she be able to live without me? I will miss her... her face... her lips... her beauty... her tenderness.... Ah! I will miss my beloved wife. Death is far more merciful than living without Juliet!"

The priest was trying to comfort him, but Romeo was

floundering in grief. And suddenly, there was a knock at the door of the cell. Lawrence turned to Romeo in panic, whispering to him, warning, "Be careful, Romeo! Get up and hide immediately. I think they came to take you out of the city! Go!"

Lawrence opened his door to find Juliet's nanny in front of him. She had almost lost her patience waiting, and without permission, she entered and closed the door behind her.

*p. 102*

"Where is he? Where is my lady's husband, Father?" the nanny asked the priest nervously.

"Here he is. He is drowned in his tears," Lawrence answered her, pointing to Romeo.

The nanny sighed and said in sorrow, "Poor man! He is like my lady." She approached him to console him.

Romeo raised his head. He was surprised to see the nanny, and a little hope returned. He asked her, "Please, tell me, where is my love? How is she? Does she think I'm a murderer? Tell me the truth, please."

"Do not worry, sir. She is devastated because of the decision of your banishment from the city, and she's crying over you profusely, and she misses you very much."

No sooner had the nanny finished her words than Romeo drew his sword as if he was about to kill himself.

Lawrence yelled angrily, "What are you doing? Are you crazy? Calm down and be a man! Your appearance is the appearance of a man but your actions are a woman's actions... weak... and defeated! What are all these emotions? Are you not ashamed of...

*p. 103*

yourself? I thought you were smart and intelligent. But you've disappointed me. Is that all you can do? Kill yourself? Oh, you coward! Have you not even considered for a moment the fate of your wife if you ever killed yourself? Is this the love you promised her? Your words are lies and nonsensical. You are about to kill that love that you are supposed to keep safe! Come on! Man up! Stand up and be happy because your beloved is fine and alive, and because you are also fine and alive, and rejoice because life continues and because your fate has deviated from death to exile. Be happy with a new life that had been given to you and with a loyal wife that is waiting for you impatiently. Enjoy a beautiful life full of blessings! Come join your beloved one; she needs you. Go before the night falls and the guards spread out! Then, you have to flee to the city of Mantua, where you will stay until we announce the news of your marriage and reconcile the two families and you can return to Verona, among us." Lawrence turned to the nanny and said, "And you, nanny, send my regards to your virtuous lady and tell her that her husband will visit her tonight!"

"What wonderful words, Father! And what precious advice! Well, I'll go and tell her," the nanny replied. Before she left, she handed the ring...

*p. 104*

to Romeo, who thanked her and breathed a sigh of relief.

The priest looked at Romeo and said to him, "Hurry up, my son, and I will tell you all the news through a messenger!"

"Agreed!" Romeo replied in gratitude.

"Goodbye."

"Goodbye."

❧ ❧ ❧

In the meantime, Lord Capulet was meeting with his wife and Lord Paris. Lord Capulet apologized to Paris. "I apologize to you, my son. I did not find the time to convince Juliet to marry you. As you know, my daughter is still mourning the death of her cousin." And, addressing his wife, he said, "Talk to your daughter and convince her to marry Paris! The wedding will be on Thursday. And tell her not to worry–we will not hold a huge party. It will be a simple party that includes only our relatives. We are still mourning our beloved Tybalt."

*p. 105*

Paris looked understanding and almost jumped with joy, thanking Juliet's parents and leaving while dreaming about Thursday.

❧ ❧ ❧

Romeo, as usual, slipped onto Juliet's balcony, where they stayed talking for hours and hours until the night was mixed with day in Romeo's mind. The poor lad was afraid of daybreak, but Juliet reassured him, "Do not worry, my love. It is still nighttime. Do not rush. Please, do not go! Romeo replied, "Okay, okay. I will not go! If you want my death, my lady!"

And they spent the night talking until dawn. The nanny interrupted them and warned, "Miss, miss! Be careful! Your mother is coming to your room! It's daytime!"

The moment of farewell came. Romeo and Juliet got up and hugged each other in sorrow. Then Romeo hurried away and disappeared from his wife's eyes, hoping to meet soon.

*p. 106*

Lady Capulet entered her daughter's room.

"How are you, my daughter? Tell me."

"Very bad, Mother," Juliet replied.

"Will you stay like this for the rest of your life, weeping and crying? Wipe away your tears and stop grieving, my daughter. Your crying will not bring Tybalt back. The biggest calamity is that his killer is still alive!" Juliet pretended to be ignorant and asked, "Who is his murderer?"

"Romeo is the murder! Romeo! "

"Romeo is not a murderer!" Juliet thought to herself, and then replied to her mother, "Oh, I wish I could avenge Tybalt myself."

"Do not worry! We will all avenge him! I will send a messenger to the city of Mantua, where he will poison and kill Romeo, and you will rejoice with the news of his death!" said Lady Capulet.

"No, I will not rejoice... I will not rejoice... until I see him... until I see him... dead ... dead like my heart when I remember my cousin. Please let me mix...

*p. 107*

the mixture myself! And so I will kill him myself!"

Her mother agreed, and she soon changed the subject, announcing the news of Juliet's wedding. "Very well, but here's the happy news now! Thursday morning... is the day of your wedding! You will marry Count Paris! Juliet was surprised by the shocking news. "What? Paris? I will never be happy with this man! I'd rather marry Romeo the murderer! Tell my father to let me at least meet him before marriage. I hardly know him."

"Here is your father, so tell him yourself!" Lady Capulet replied angrily.

Lord Capulet entered followed by the nanny. He sat

down to console his daughter. Then he turned to his wife and asked her if she had told Juliet about the wedding. Lady Capulet told him that Juliet did not approve the news.

Lord Capulet lost his temper and shouted at Juliet, "What? You disagree? You are so ungrateful! You should be happy with this great union! You are supposed to be thankful, you spoiled girl! Are you not ashamed of yourself? Come now, and get ready for your wedding...

*p. 108*

On Thursday, you will go willingly to St. Peter's Church, or I will force you to go. Do you understand? And now, get out of my face!"

Juliet broke into tears while the nanny tried to defend her and convince her parents to listen to her, but Lord Capulet and his wife refused sternly. Before they left Juliet's room, her father said to her, "Either you will obey my orders or I will throw you onto the streets where you will die from hunger, coldness, and poverty. Make a choice!"

He went away leaving Juliet crying bitterly, and Lady Capulet followed him.

Juliet hugged her nanny, asking her for help. The nanny felt sorry for her. She hugged her and asked, "What do you think about marrying Paris? Romeo is far away from you, and Paris is a handsome, classy young man who will make you happy."

The words of the nanny shocked Juliet. She felt like the whole world was against her. She pulled herself together and said, "Well, you're right. I'll go to Father Lawrence and confess to him all my sins... Please tell my mother."

*p. 109*

"Okay, my lady," the nanny answered enthusiastically and got up quickly.

As for Juliet, she thought to herself, "What an evil soul! May the angels curse her! She wants me to betray my husband! What a hypocrite! I will not tell her anything! I will go to Friar Lawrence. Perhaps he will find a solution for my miserable life; otherwise... otherwise, I will end it myself."

# اَلْفَصْلُ السَّابِعُ

تَوَجَّهَ باريسُ مُسْرِعًا إِلَى الْقِسِّيسِ لورنْسَ لِيُعْلِنَ لَهُ خَبَرَ زِفافِهِ بِجوليِيتْ فَسأَلَهُ لورنْسُ في تَعَجُّبٍ: "يَوْمَ الْخَميسِ؟ لِمَ كُلُّ هَذِهِ السُّرْعَةِ يا بُنَيَّ؟"

"هَكَذا قَرَّرَ السَّيِّدُ كابوليتْ. فَكَما تَعْلَمُ يا أَبَتِ جوليِيتْ لا تَزالُ حَزينَةً عَلَى رَحيلِ ابْنِ عَمِّها تَيْبالْتْ وَهِيَ الآنَ مُحْتاجَةٌ لِمَنْ يُسانِدُها وَيواسيها... إِنَّها مُحْتاجَةٌ لي!" أَجابَهُ باريسُ في حَماسٍ.

دَخَلَتْ عَلَيْهِما جوليِيتْ وَقَدْ بانَ التَّعَبُ وَالْحُزْنُ عَلَى وَجْهِها. لَمْ يَرُقْ

لَها أَبَدًا وُجودُ باريس، فاستَأْذَنَتْ مِنْهُ بِلُطْفٍ لِيَتْرُكَها وَحْدَها مَعَ لورِنْس لِكَيْ تَسْتَطيعَ أَنْ تَعْتَرِفَ لَهُ بِأَخْطائِها. اِبْتَسَمَ لَها باريس وَقَبَّلَها قائِلًا: "حَسَنًا سَأُغادِرُ... نَلْتَقي يَوْمَ الْخَميسِ... سَأُوقِظُكِ في الصَّباحِ الْباكِرِ... إِلَى اللِّقاءِ حَبيبَتي!"

بَقِيَتْ جولييت لِوَحْدِها مَعَ لورِنْس تُعَبِّرُ لَهُ عَنْ حُزْنِها الشَّديد. كانَ الْقِسّيسُ يُحاوِلُ إيجادَ حَلٍّ وَلَكِنَّ الْحُلولَ بَدَتْ مُنْعَدِمَةً، فَمَوْعِدُ الزَّفافِ قَدِ اقْتَرَبَ وَلا شَيْءَ يُمْكِنُ تَأْجيلُهُ.

وَفي لَحْظَةِ يَأْسٍ، أَخْرَجَتْ جولييت خِنْجَرًا وَقالَتْ لِلورِنْس: "عَلَيْكَ أَنْ تَجِدَ لي حَلًّا يا أَبَتِ فَأَنْتَ الَّذي عَقَدْتَ قِرانَنا وَأَنْتَ الَّذي بارَكْتَ زَواجَنا وَالآنَ يَجِبُ أَنْ تُساعِدَنا... وَإِلَّا... فَسَأُساعِدُ نَفْسي بِهَذا الْخِنْجَرِ! فَالْمَوْتُ أَرْفَقُ بي إِنِ انْعَدَمَتْ كُلُّ الْحُلولِ!"

أُصيبَ الْقِسّيسُ بِالْفَزَعِ لِرُؤْيَةِ الْخِنْجَرِ فَصَرَخَ بِها: "اِنْتَظِري، اِنْتَظِري يا اِبْنَتي أَرْجوكِ! سَوْفَ نَجِدُ حَلًّا!"

هَدَأَتْ جولييت قَليلًا وَسَأَلَتْهُ: "وَما هُوَ هَذا الْحَلُّ؟ أَخْبِرْني يا أَبَتِ!"

"حَسَنًا، إِنْ كُنْتِ لا تَخافينَ مِنَ الْمَوْتِ فَلَدَيَّ الْحَلُّ الْمُناسِبُ...

وَلَكِنَّهُ لَيْسَ حَلًّا سَهْلًا أَبَدًا... فَهُوَ يَتَطَلَّبُ جُرْأَةً وَشَجَاعَةً مِنْكِ، وَهُوَ قَرِيبٌ جِدًّا مِنْ فِكْرَةِ الْمَوْتِ... لِذَا قُولِي لِي، هَلْ أَنْتِ مُسْتَعِدَّةٌ... أَمْ لَا؟"

"نَعَمْ! مُسْتَعِدَّةٌ! وَلَسْتُ خَائِفَةً يَا أَبَتِ! سَأَفْعَلُ الْمُسْتَحِيلَ مِنْ أَجْلِ زَوْجِي الْعَزِيزِ!" أَجَابَتْهُ جُولِييتْ بِكُلِّ ثِقَةٍ فِي نَفْسِهَا.

"حَسَنًا، حَسَنًا، إِذَنْ عُودِي الآنَ إِلَى مَنْزِلِكِ وَتَظَاهَرِي بِالْفَرَحِ وَقُولِي لَهُمْ أَنَّكِ قَبِلْتِ بِبَارِيسَ زَوْجًا لَكِ وَشَرِيكًا لِحَيَاتِكِ... وَغَدًا، أَيْ يَوْمُ الْأَرْبِعَاءِ فِي اللَّيْلِ، سَتَبْقِينَ وَحْدَكِ فِي غُرْفَتِكِ، لَا تَتْرُكِي الْمُرَبِّيَةَ مَعَكِ! اتَّفَقْنَا؟ وَعِنْدَهَا، سَتَأْخُذِينَ هَذَا التِّرْيَاقَ (وَأَشَارَ الرَّاهِبُ لُورِنْس إِلَى تِرْيَاقٍ) وَسَتُخْلِطِينَ مُحْتَوَيَاتَهُ بِسَائِلٍ وَسَتَشْرَبِينَهُ. وَحِينَهَا، سَتُغْمَضُ عَيْنَاكِ وَسَتَتَوَقَّفُ دَقَّاتُ قَلْبِكِ وَسَيُصْبِحُ جَسَدُكِ بَارِدًا جِدًّا وَسَتَتَوَقَّفِينَ عَنِ التَّنَفُّسِ، وَلَوْنُكِ سَيُصْبِحُ شَاحِبًا وَسَتَعْجَزِينَ عَنِ التَّحَرُّكِ، وَسَتَبْدِينَ كَجُثَّةٍ هَامِدَةٍ، وَسَتَظَلِّينَ هَكَذَا أَكْثَرَ مِنْ يَوْمٍ. ثُمَّ سَتَسْتَيْقِظِينَ يَوْمَ الْخَمِيسِ. سَيَكْتَشِفُ الْجَمِيعُ خَبَرَ مَوْتِكِ وَسَيَحْزَنُونَ، ثُمَّ سَيُلْبِسُونَكِ أَبْهَى حُلَّةٍ وَسَيَضَعُونَكِ فِي النَّعْشِ وَيَجْلِبُونَكِ إِلَى مَقْبَرَةِ عَائِلَةِ كَابُولِيتْ، وَأَكُونُ أَنَا قَدْ أَرْسَلْتُ رَسُولًا إِلَى رُومِيُو لِأُخْبِرَهُ بِخُطَّتِنَا وَسَوْفَ نَلْتَحِقُ بِكِ هُنَالِكَ، وَنَنْتَظِرُكِ حَتَّى تَسْتَفِيقِي مِنَ الْغَيْبُوبَةِ

وَعِنْدَها... سَيَحْمِلُكِ زَوْجُكِ إِلَى مَدِينَةِ مَنْتُوا. هذا هُوَ حَلِّي الوَحيدُ يا ابْنَتي..."

عادَ الأَمَلُ إِلَى قَلْبِ جولييت مِنْ جَديدٍ، فَافْتَكَّتِ التِّرْياقَ مِنْ يدِ لورِنْس وَأَجابَتْهُ: "مُوافِقَةٌ يا أَبَتِ! شُكْرًا لَكَ!" تَمَنَّى لَها القِسِّيسُ حَظًّا مُوَفَّقًا في تَنْفيذِ الخُطَّةِ، وَوَدَّعا بَعْضَهُما، وَشَرَعَ يَكْتُبُ رِسالَةً لِيُرْسِلَها إِلَى روميو مَعَ راهِبٍ صَديقٍ لَهُ.

في تِلْكَ الأَثْناءِ، كانَ جَميعُ أَفْرادِ عائِلَةِ جولييت مُنْهَمِكينَ في إِعْدادِ حَفْلَةِ الزَّواجِ، وَتَوْزيعِ الدَّعَواتِ، وَطَبْخِ الْمَأْكولاتِ الشَّهِيَّةِ. دَخَلَتْ عَلَيْهِمْ جولييت مَسْرورَةً ضاحِكَةً مِثْلَما أَوْصاها لورِنْس، فَسَعِدَتِ الْمُرَبِّيَةُ والسَّيِّدَةُ كابوليت لِرُؤْيَتِها سَعيدَةً وَأَسْرَعَتا لِإِعْدادِ مَلازِمِها مِنْ ثِيابٍ وَمُجَوْهَراتٍ، أَمَّا السَّيِّدُ كابوليت فَالْتَحَقَ بِباريس لِيُساعِدَهُ أَيْضًا.

وَفي الغُرْفَةِ، الْتَفَتَتْ جولييت إِلَى مُرَبِّيَتِها وَقالَتْ لَها بِلُطْفٍ: "أَرْجوكِ مُرَبِّيَتي، دَعيني لِوَحْدي هَذِهِ اللَّيْلَةَ... يَجِبُ أَنْ أُصَلِّي وَأَدْعوَ كَثيرًا لِكَيْ تُغْفَرَ ذُنوبي."

"حَسَنًا آنِسَتي، كَما تُريدينَ." أجابَتْها المُرَبِّيَةُ وغادَرَتْ غُرْفَةَ جولييت لِتَلْتَحِقَ بِالسَّيِّدَةِ كابوليت.

عِنْدَما وَجَدَتْ جولييت نَفْسَها وَحيدَةً بغُرْفَتِها، إنْتابَها شُعورٌ غَريبٌ مَمْزوجٌ بِالْخَوْفِ وَالرِّيبَةِ. فَهِيَ لَمْ تَعْتَدِ الْبَقاءَ بِمُفْرَدِها أوِ الْإقْدامَ عَلى خُطَطٍ بِدونِ مُرَبِّيَتِها، وَبَدَأتِ الْأسْئِلَةُ تُراوِدُ ذِهْنَها: "ماذا لَوْ أنَّ الْخَليطَ لَمْ يُعْطِ مَفْعولَهُ؟ ماذا لَوْ أنَّ لورِنْس أرادَ فِعْلًا قَتْلي؟ لا! هَذا غَيرُ مُمْكِنٍ! فَهُوَ رَجُلُ دينٍ... وَلَنْ يُقْدِمَ عَلى قَتْلي! ماذا لَوِ اسْتَيْقَظْتُ قَبْلَ وُصولِ روميو؟ هَلْ سَأخْتَنِقُ في الْمَقْبَرَةِ؟ هَلْ سَأموتُ مُخْتَنِقَةً؟ أوْ سَأموتُ خَوْفًا مِنْ رُؤْيَةِ الْأمْواتِ وَالْأشْباحِ الَّتي سَتُحاصِرُني مِنْ كُلِّ مَكانٍ؟ سَوْفَ أجِدُ جُثَّةَ تيبالْت مُتَعَفِّنَةً... سَوْفَ أرى أشْياءَ مُرْعِبَةً... وَسَوْفَ أشْتَمُّ رَوائِحَ كَريهَةً... وَسَوْفَ أسْمَعُ أصْواتًا مُخيفَةً... وَسَوْفَ أجَنُّ مِنْ هَوْلِ الْمَشْهَدِ... تيبالْت! لا! روميو! روميو! ها أنا أشْرَبُ هَذا الْمَشْروبَ مِنْ أجْلِكَ!" وَشَرِبَتِ الْخَليطَ كُلَّهُ وَسَقَطَتْ عَلى سَريرِها.

أمَّا السَّيِّدَةُ كابوليت وَزَوْجُها وَالْمُرَبِّيَةُ فَلَمْ يَغْمَضْ لَهُمْ جَفْنٌ، بَلْ ظَلّوا

يُعِدُّونَ لَوازِمَ الْحَفْلِ. وَمَعَ طُلوعِ الْفَجْرِ، أَمَرَ السَّيِّدُ كابوليت الْمُرَبِّيَةَ أَنْ تَذْهَبَ إِلَى غُرْفَةِ جولييت وَتوقِظَها لِتُساعِدَها عَلَى تَجْهيزِ نَفْسِها. فَأَسْرَعَتِ الْمُرَبِّيَةُ نَحْوَ جولييت: "آنِسَتي! آنِسَتي! هَيّا اسْتَيْقِظي! فَهَذا يَوْمُكِ! يا إِلَهي! إِنَّها تَغُطُّ في نَوْمٍ عَميقٍ... آنِسَتي! انْهَضي!" وَكانَتِ الْمُرَبِّيَةُ تَقْتَرِبُ شَيْئًا فَشَيْئًا مِنْ جولييت وَفَجْأَةً، اِكْتَشَفَتْ أَنَّها لا تَتَحَرَّكُ. حاوَلَتْ إيقاظَها جاهِدَةً لَكِنْ دونَ جَدْوَى، فَصَرَخَتْ في ذُعْرٍ: "آنِسَتي! آنِسَتي! آنِسَتي! اَلنَّجْدَةَ! آنِسَتي قَدْ فارَقَتِ الْحَياةَ! يا إِلَهي! مُصيبَةٌ! هَذِهِ مُصيبَةٌ!"

هَرَعَتِ السَّيِّدَةُ كابوليت إِلَى غُرْفَةِ جولييت وَوَراؤُها زَوْجُها لِيَكْتَشِفا ابْنَتَهُما جُثَّةً هامِدَةً! صُعِقا مِنَ الْمَشْهَدِ وانهارا، وَهُنا دَخَلَ عَلَيْهِمِ الْقِسّيسُ لورِنْسْ بِرِفْقَةِ باريس وَبَعْضِ الْموسيقيّينَ.

"هَلْ عَروسُنا جاهِزَةٌ لِلذَّهابِ إِلَى الْكَنيسَةِ؟" سَأَلَ لورِنْسْ.

"نَعَمْ... جاهِزَةٌ! جاهِزَةٌ... لِلذَّهابِ... وَلَكِنْ... وَلَكِنْ... دونَ عَوْدَةٍ!" أَجابَهُ السَّيِّدُ كابوليت في حُزْنٍ، ثُمَّ نَظَرَ إِلَى باريس قائِلًا: "يا بُنَيِّ! اَلْمَوْتُ سَرَقَ لَكَ عَروسَكَ!"

اِنْهارَ الْجَميعُ حُزْنًا في حينِ حاوَلَ لورِنْسْ تَهْدِئَتَهُمْ قائِلًا: "اِهْدَؤوا!

أَرْجوكُمْ، اِهْدَؤوا! فَبُكاؤُكُمْ هَذا لَنْ يُعيدَ جولييتْ... وَصُراخُكُمْ لَنْ يُرْجِعَها... ما كُلُّ هَذا النَّحيبِ؟ إنَّ جولييتْ الآنَ في مَكانٍ أَفْضَلَ بِكَثيرٍ وَأَجْمَلَ... وَسَتَنْعَمُ بِحَياةٍ أُخْرى نَجْهَلُ أَسْرارَها... هَيَّا امْسَحوا دُموعَكُمْ أَرْجوكُمْ وَاحْمِلوها في نَعْشِها إلى الْكَنيسَةِ."

خَبَّأَ الموسيقيُّونَ آلاتَهُمْ وَعادوا أَعْقابَهُمْ. في حينِ تَوَجَّهَ السَّيِّدُ كابوليتْ وَزَوْجَتُهُ وَباريسْ وَالْكاهِنِ لِإِعْدادِ مَراسيمِ الدَّفْنِ.

# Vocabulary

### p. 122

| | |
|---|---|
| أَعْلَنَ [4s] to announce | تَعَبٌ (أَتْعابٌ) fatigue |
| رَحيلٌ departure; *here:* demise | راقَ [1h3] (رَوْقٌ) to please, delight |
| سانَدَ [3s] to support | |
| بانَ [1h2] (بَيانٌ) to appear, be visible | |

### p. 123

| | |
|---|---|
| بِلُطْفٍ gently, kindly | أَجَّلَ [2s(a)] (تَأْجيلٌ) to delay |
| خَطَأٌ (أَخْطاءٌ) error, mistake, sin | خِنْجَرٌ (خَناجِرُ) dagger |
| أَيْقَظَ [4a2] (إيقاظٌ) to awaken, rouse | اِنْعَدَمَ [7s] to be lacking, non-existent |
| أَوْجَدَ [4a1] (إيجادٌ) to produce | خافَ مِنْ [1h1] (خَوْفٌ) to be afraid of |
| مُنْعَدِمٌ lacking, non-existent | |

### p. 124

| | |
|---|---|
| تَطَلَّبَ [5s] to require | أَغْمَضَ [4s] to close |
| شَجاعَةٌ bravery | دَقَّةٌ (heart)beat |
| لِذا so, then, thus | بارِدٌ cold |
| مُسْتَحيلٌ impossible, unthinkable | تَنَفُّسٌ breathing |
| شَريكٌ (شُرَكاءُ) partner | هامِدٌ lifeless, motionless |
| تِرْياقٌ (تَرايِيقُ) potion | حَزِنَ [1s4] (حُزْنٌ) to grieve, mourn |
| مُحْتَوَياتٌ *pl.* contents | أَلْبَسَ [4s] to dress |
| سائِلٌ (سَوائِلُ) liquid | بَهِيٌّ (أَبْهِياءُ) splendid, magnificent; *elative* أَبْهَى |

حُلَّةٌ garment
نَعْشٌ (نُعوشٌ) coffin
جَلَبَ (جَلْبٌ) [1s3] to bring
مَقْبَرَةٌ (مَقابِرُ) cemetery

خُطَّةٌ (خُطَطٌ) plan, project
اِسْتَفاقَ [10h] to wake up
غَيْبوبَةٌ coma

*p. 125*

وَعِنْدَها at which time
اِفْتَكَّ [8g1] to snatch away, grab
مُوَفَّقٌ successful
نَفَّذَ (تَنْفيذٌ) [2s] to implement, carry out
مُنْهَمِكٌ engaged, engrossed, busy
إِعْدادٌ preparation
وَزَّعَ (تَوْزيعٌ) [2s] to distribute
دَعْوَةٌ invitation
مَأكولاتٌ *pl.* food

شَهِيٌّ appetizing
مَسْرورٌ pleased, happy
مِثْلَما as, like
أَوْصى [4d(b)] to advise
ثِيابٌ *pl.* clothes
مُجَوْهَراتٌ *pl.* jewelery
صَلّى [2d] to pray
غُفِرَ (مَغْفِرَةٌ/غُفْرانٌ) [1s2] to be forgiven
ذَنْبٌ (ذُنوبٌ) sin, offense

*p. 126*

اِنْتابَ [8h1] to come over, attack
شُعورٌ (شُعورٌ) feeling
مَمْزوجٌ mixed
رِيبَةٌ (رَيْبٌ) doubt, suspicion
اِعْتادَ [8h1] to be accustomed to
بِمُفْرَدِهِ alone
راوَدَ [3s] to approach, accost; to haunt
خَليطٌ (خُلَطاءُ) mixture
مَفْعولٌ (مَفاعيلُ) effect, impact
اِخْتَنَقَ [8s1] to suffocate

شَبَحٌ (أَشْباحٌ) ghost, spirit
حاصَرَ [3s] to besiege, haunt
مُتَعَفِّنٌ decayed, rotten
مُرْعِبٌ horrific, dreadful
اِشْتَمَّ [8g1] to smell
كَريهٌ foul, disgusting
مُخيفٌ scary, frightening
هَوْلٌ (أَهْوالٌ) fright, terror
مَشْهَدٌ (مَشاهِدُ) scene
مَشْروبٌ drink, beverage
جَفْنٌ (جُفونٌ) eyelid

*p. 127*

أَعَدَّ [4g] to prepare

لَوازِمُ *pl.* necessities

أَمَرَ (أَمْرٌ) [1s3(a)] to command, order
حَضَّرَ (تَحْضِيرٌ) [2s] to prepare
إلاهي My God!
غَطَّ في (غَطّ) [1g3] to plunge into

ذُعْرٌ panic
النَّجْدَةَ! Help!
عَروسٌ (عرائسُ) bride
عَوْدَةٌ return(ing)
سَرَقَ (سَرِقَةٌ) [1s2] to steal

*p. 128*

أعادَ [4h] to bring back, return
صُراخٌ screaming
أَرْجَعَ [4s] to bring back, return
نَحيبٌ wailing
نَعِمَ (نَعْمَةٌ) [1s4] to live in luxury

جَهِلَ (جَهْلٌ/جَهالَةٌ) [1s4] to be ignorant of
خَبَّأَ [2s(c)] to hide
عادَ أَعْقابَهُ (عَوْدَةٌ/عَوْدٌ) [1h3] to turn back, retrace one's steps,
مَراسِمُ *pl.* ceremony

## Translation

*p. 122*

Paris rushed to Friar Lawrence to tell him the news of his wedding to Juliet. Lawrence asked him in wonder, "On Thursday? Why the rush, my son?"

"This is what Lord Capulet has decided. As you know, Father, Juliet is still sad about the death of her cousin Tybalt, and now she needs someone to support her and to console her. She needs me!" Paris responded excitedly.

Juliet came in. Her face was tired and sad. She didn't appreciate...

*p. 123*

Paris's presence at all. So she kindly asked him to leave her alone with Lawrence so that she could confess her sins to him. Paris smiled at her and said, "All right, I'll leave. We'll meet on Thursday. I'll wake you up early in the morning. Goodbye, my darling!"

Juliet remained alone with Lawrence. She expressed to him her deep sorrow. The priest was trying to come up with a solution but solutions seemed to fade. The wedding date was approaching and nothing could postpone it.

In a moment of despair, Juliet drew a knife and said to Lawrence, "You have to find a solution for me, Father. You are the one who married us, and who blessed our marriage, and now you have to help us. Otherwise, I will help myself with this dagger. Death is more merciful for me if there are no solutions!"

The priest was horrified to see the dagger and screamed, "Wait, wait, my daughter, please! We will find a solution!"

Juliet calmed down a little and asked him, "What is this solution? Tell me, Father!"

"Well, if you do not fear death, I have the right solution...

*p. 124*

for you. But it is not an easy solution at all. It requires bravery and courage on your part, and it is very close to the idea of death. So tell me, are you ready... or not?"

"Yes! Ready! I'm not afraid, Father! I will do anything for my dear husband!" Juliet replied with confidence.

"Very well. Then go back to your house now, and pretend to be happy and tell them that you have accepted Paris as your husband and partner. Tomorrow, Wednesday at night, you will be alone in your room. Stay away from your nanny! Agreed? Then you will take this potion." Friar Lawrence pointed to a potion. "And you will mix its contents with a liquid and you drink it. And then your eyes will close, your heart will stop beating, your body will become very cold, you will stop breathing, your color will become pale, you will be unable to move. You will look like a lifeless corpse, and you will stay like this for over a day. Then you will wake up on Thursday. Everyone will learn of your death and will grieve. Then they'll dress you in splendid garments, put you in a coffin, and bring you to the Capulet family cemetery. In the meantime, I will be sending a messenger to Romeo to inform him of our plan, and we will join you there and wait for you to wake up from your deep sleep,...

*p. 125*

at which point your husband will take you to the city of

Mantua. This is the only solution that I have, my daughter."

Hope returned to Juliet's heart again. She snatched away the potion from Lawrence and told him, "I agree. Thank you, Father!" The priest wished her good luck in carrying out the plan and they bid each other farewell. He began to write a letter to Romeo that he would send to him with a monk friend of his.

Meanwhile, all members of Juliet's family were busy preparing for the wedding party, distributing invitations, and cooking delicious meals. Juliet came in, happy and laughing as Lawrence had advised her to do. The nanny and Lady Capulet were pleased to see her happy and hurried to prepare her clothes and jewelry. As for Lord Capulet, he joined Paris to help him, as well.

In her room, Juliet turned to her nanny and said gently, "Please, nanny, leave me alone tonight. I must pray a lot so that my sins will be forgiven."

*p. 126*

"Okay, my lady, as you wish," the nanny answered her and left Juliet's room to join Lady Capulet.

When Juliet found herself alone in her room, she felt a strange feeling mixed with fear and doubt. She was not used to staying alone or making plans without her nanny. Questions began to hover over her mind. "What if the mixture had no effect? What if Lawrence really wanted to kill me? No! This is not possible! He is a man of God... and he would not dare kill me! What if I wake up before Romeo arrives? Will I suffocate in the tomb? Will I suffocate to death? Or will I die of fear of seeing the dead and ghosts that will haunt me from everywhere? I will find the rotten corpse of Tybalt... I will see horrible things... I will smell disgusting odors... I will hear scary sounds... I will go crazy from the horrible sights. Tybalt! No! Romeo! Romeo!

Romeo! Here I drink this for you!" She drank the whole mixture and fell onto her bed.

ஒ ஒ ஒ

Lady Capulet and her husband and the nanny did not sleep a wink, rather they kept...

Preparing for the ceremony. As dawn approached, Lord Capulet ordered the nanny to go to Juliet's room and wake her up to help her get ready. The nanny rushed towards Juliet. "Miss! Miss! Come on, wake up! This is your day! Oh my God! She is in a deep sleep... Miss! Get up! The nanny was slowly approaching Juliet and suddenly, she discovered that she was not moving. She tried hard to wake her up but in vain. She screamed in panic, "Miss! Miss! Miss!... Help! My Lady has died! Oh my God! Calamity! This is a disaster!"

Lady Capulet rushed to Juliet's room, followed by her husband, to find their daughter a stiff corpse! They were shocked by the scene and collapsed. And then came Friar Lawrence accompanied by Paris and some musicians.

"Is our bride ready to go to church?" Lawrence asked.

"Yes... ready! Ready... to go... but... but... without coming back!" Lord Capulet answered in sadness, and then he looked at Paris saying, "My son! Death has stolen from you your bride!"

Everyone collapsed in sadness while Lawrence tried to calm them down. He said, "Calm down!

Please, calm down! This crying will not bring Juliet back. Your screaming will not bring her back. What is all this wailing? Juliet is now in a much better and nicer place. She will live another life, the secrets of which we do not know.

Wipe your tears and take her in her coffin to the church."

The musicians concealed their instruments and went back. Meanwhile, Lord Capulet, his wife, Paris, and the priest went to prepare for the funeral.

# اَلْفَصْلُ الثَّامِنُ

اسْتَيْقَظَ روميو مِنْ حُلْمٍ راوَدَهُ في اللَّيْلِ، يَبْدو أَنَّهُ لَمْ يَفْهَمْهُ إِنْ كانَ حُلْمًا جَميلًا أَمْ كابوسًا مُرْعِبًا. كانَ يَحْلُمُ وَكَأَنَّهُ قَدْ فارَقَ الْحَياةَ... فاقْتَرَبَتْ مِنْهُ جوليِيتْ وَقَبَّلَتْهُ... فَأَعادَتْ لَهُ أَنْفاسَهُ وَأَحْيَتْهُ مِنْ جَديدٍ...

وَبَيْنَما كانَ يُحاوِلُ تَحْليلَ حُلْمِهِ هَذا، دَخَلَ عَلَيْهِ خادِمُهُ **بِالتَّهَزازِ** فَانْقَضَّ عَلَيْهِ روميو بِالْأَسْئِلَةِ: "هَلْ مِنْ أَخْبارٍ جَديدَةٍ مِنْ فيرونا؟ كَيْفَ حالُ زَوْجَتي؟ هَلْ هِيَ جَيِّدَة؟ أَخْبِرْني أَرْجوكَ!"

"ماذا تُرِيدُنِي أَنْ أُخْبِرَكَ سَيِّدِي؟ أُخْبِرُكَ أَنَّ زَوْجَتَكَ قَدْ وَارَى جِسْمَها التُّرَابُ؟ أَمْ أُخْبِرُكَ أَنَّ رُوحَ زَوْجَتِكَ الآنَ تَطْفُو مَعَ الْمَلَائِكَةِ فَوْقَ مَقْبَرَةِ كَابُولِيتْ؟ نَعَمْ! لَقَدْ مَاتَتْ جُولْيِيتْ... وَشَهِدْتُ عَلَى مَرَاسِمِ دَفْنِهَا... وَإِنَّ قَلْبِي يَتَقَطَّعُ أَلَمًا عَلَيْكَ يَا سَيِّدِي... وَلَكِنْ مَاذَا عَسَايَ أَنْ أَفْعَلَ؟ إِنَّنِي مُجْبَرٌ لِأَنْقُلَ لَكَ الْخَبَرَ... أَعْتَذِرُ مِنْكَ سَيِّدِي... أَرْجُوكَ سَامِحْنِي..."

كَادَ رُومْيُو يُجَنُّ مِنْ هَوْلِ الْخَبَرِ. إِصْفَرَّ وَجْهُهُ وَاحْمَرَّتْ عَيْنَاهُ وَشَعَرَ بِالْعَالَمِ يَهْوِي مِنْ حَوْلِهِ، وَبِأَحْلَامِهِ تَتَهَجَّرُ أَمَامَهُ، وَبِآمَالِهِ تَتَحَطَّمُ فَوْقَ رَأْسِهِ، إِلَّا أَنَّهُ حَاوَلَ التَّمَاسُكَ قَلِيلًا وَطَلَبَ مِنْ خَادِمِهِ أَنْ يُحْضِرَ لَهُ وَرَقًا وَحِبْرًا لِيَكْتُبَ رِسَالَةً، وَجَوَادًا لِيَرْكَبَهُ. فَذَهَبَ بِالْتِهْزَازٍ مُمْتَثِلًا لِأَوَامِرِ رُومْيُو وَبَقِيَ هَذَا الْأَخِيرُ فِي حُجْرَتِهِ وَحِيدًا يَبْكِي زَوْجَتَهُ. وَفَجْأَةً، رَاوَدَتْهُ فِكْرَةٌ، فَخَرَجَ مُسْرِعًا وَاتَّجَهَ إِلَى صَيْدَلِيٍّ فَقِيرِ الْحَالِ يُتْقِنُ إِعْدَادَ أَدْوِيَةٍ وَعَقَاقِيرَ سَامَّةٍ. كَانَ بَيْعُ هَذِهِ الْعَقَاقِيرِ مَمْنُوعًا بَاتًّا فِي الْمَدِينَةِ، وَكَانَ عِقَابُ كُلِّ مَنْ يَبِيعُهَا الْمَوْتَ، إِلَّا أَنَّ رُومْيُو أَقْنَعَهُ بِالْقِطَعِ النَّقْدِيَّةِ الذَّهَبِيَّةِ، فَأَخَذَ مِنْهُ جُرْعَةً سَامَّةً وَانْصَرَفَ مُتَّجِهَا إِلَى قَبْرِ جُولْيِيتْ.

وَفِي هَذِهِ الْأَثْنَاءِ، قَابَلَ الرَّاهِبُ لورنس صَدِيقَهُ الرَّاهِبَ دُجون وَسَأَلَهُ إِنْ كَانَ قَدْ أَوْصَلَ الرِّسَالَةَ إِلَى رومِيو فَأَجَابَهُ دُجون مُتَأَسِّفًا: "لا... لَمْ أَقْدِرْ عَلَى إِيصَالِها... فَقَدْ مَنَعوني أَعْوَانُ الصِّحَّةِ مِنَ الْعُبورِ إِلَى مَنْتوا أَنا وَرَاهِبٍ آخَرَ وَذَلِكَ بِسَبَبِ وَبَاءٍ خَطِيرٍ أَصَابَ الْعَدِيدَ مِنَ الْأَشْخَاصِ، وَقَدْ ظَنُّوا أَنَّنَا كُنَّا فِي مَنْزِلٍ اِنْتَشَرَ فِيهِ هَذَا الْوَبَاءُ... فَها أَنا عَالِقٌ هُنَا وَها هِيَ رِسَالَتُكَ." وَمَدَّ بِالرِّسَالَةِ إِلَى لورنس الَّذِي أَصَابَهُ الْهَلَعُ لِسَمَاعِ هَذَا الْخَبَرِ السَّيِّءِ. فَقَرَّرَ الذَّهَابَ إِلَى الْمَقْبَرَةِ كَيْ لا تَجِدَ جولييت نَفْسَها وَحِيدَةً عِنْدَما تَسْتَيْقِظُ، وَلَكِنْ قَبْلَ ذَلِكَ شَرَعَ يَكْتُبُ رِسَالَةً جَدِيدَةً إِلَى رومِيو لِيوافِيهِ بِالْأَخْبَارِ الْجَدِيدَةِ.

عِنْدَما أَرْسَى اللَّيْلُ ظَلامَهُ عَلَى مَدِينَةِ فيرونا، ذَهَبَ باريس بِرِفْقَةِ خَادِمِهِ إِلَى الْمَقْبَرَةِ حَامِلاً وُرودًا عَلَى أَمَلِ أَنْ يُخَفِّفَ عَنْ مُصِيبَتِهِ قَلِيلاً. نَثَرَ الْوُرودَ عَلَى قَبْرِ جولييت وَظَلَّ يَبْكِيها بِحُرْقَةٍ. وَفَجْأَةً، قَاطَعَهُ خَادِمُهُ مُرْتَبِكًا: "سَيِّدي! سَيِّدي! انْتَبِهْ هُنَالِكَ مَنْ يَقْتَرِبُ مِنَّا وَبِيَدِهِ مَشْعَلٌ!" فَنَهَضَ باريس وَاخْتَبَأَ مَعَ خَادِمِهِ لِمُرَاقَبَةِ ما يَحْصُلُ. وَإِذا بِرومِيو يَقْتَرِبُ شَيْئًا فَشَيْئًا وَبِرِفْقَتِهِ بالْتَّهَزَارْ.

وَقَفَ رومِيو بِقُرْبِ ضَرِيحِ جولييت وَأَعْطَى رِسَالَةً إِلَى بالْتَّهَزَارْ قَائِلاً: "خُذْ هَذِهِ الرِّسَالَةَ وَغَدًا صَبَاحًا يَجِبُ أَنْ تُسَلِّمَها إِلَى وَالِدي...

وَالآنَ سَأَنْزِلُ إِلَى قَبْرِ جولييت لِأَحْتَضِنَها... وَأُوَدِّعَها... لِذَلِكَ فاحْذَرْ أَنْ تَمْنَعَنِي عَنْ ذَلِكَ وَإِلَّا فَسَأَقْتُلُكَ... هَلْ هَذَا مَفْهُومٌ؟ وَالآنَ اذْهَبْ وَاغْرُبْ عَنْ وَجْهِي!"

ذَهَبَ الْخَادِمُ إِلَّا أَنَّهُ اخْتَبَأَ لِيُرَاقِبَ رومْيو عَنْ بُعْدٍ فِي حِينِ شَرَعَ هَذَا الأَخِيرُ فِي فَتْحِ ضَرِيحِ جولييت مُخَاطِبًا نَفْسَهُ: "أَيُّهَا الْمَوْتُ الشِّرِّيرُ... لَقَدْ سَلَبْتَنِي أَغْلَى مَا أَمْلِكُ وَالآنَ هَا أَنَا أُسَلِّمُ لَكِ نَفْسِي أَيْضًا...".

سَمِعَهُ باريس فَخَرَجَ مِنْ مَخْبَئِهِ فِي ذُهُولٍ وَصَاحَ: "أَيُّهَا النَّذْلُ الْحَقِيرُ مُنْتِغْيو! أَتَأْخُذُ بِثَأْرِكَ مِنَ الأَمْوَاتِ؟ أَنْتَ مَجْنُونٌ! تَعَالَ مَعِي الآنَ! وَحَالًا! يَجِبُ أَنْ تُعَاقَبَ عَلَى فِعْلِكَ الشَّنِيعِ! يَجِبُ أَنْ تَمُوتَ!"

نَظَرَ إِلَيْهِ رومْيو بِحِقْدٍ وَأَجَابَهُ: "أَرْجُوكَ ابْتَعِدْ لَا أُرِيدُ ارْتِكَابَ جَرِيمَةٍ أُخْرَى... هَيَّا ابْتَعِدْ عَنِّي حَالًا!"

رَفَضَ باريس الِابْتِعَادَ عَنْ رومْيو فَبَدَآ فِي شِجَارٍ عَنِيفٍ انْتَهَى بِمَقْتَلِ باريس. هَرَعَ خَادِمُ هَذَا الأَخِيرِ لِيَجْلِبَ الْحُرَّاسَ لِحِمَايَةِ سَيِّدِهِ حَيْثُ لَمْ يَتَفَطَّنْ أَنَّ سَيِّدَهُ قَدْ مَاتَ.

أَمَّا رُومْيُو، فَقَدْ عَادَ لِفَتْحِ قَبْرِ جُولِييت. نَظَرَ إِلَى وَجْهِهَا فَأَجْهَشَ بِالْبُكَاءِ قَائِلًا: "زَوْجَتِي الْحَبِيبَةُ مَا أَجْمَلَكِ! الْمَوْتُ الْتَقَطَ أَنْفَاسَكِ... لَكِنْ عَجَزَ عَنْ أَخْذِ جَمَالِكِ... لَا تَخَافِي... سَوْفَ أَبْقَى جَانِبَكِ وَلَنْ أُغَادِرَكِ... سَوْفَ أَبْقَى هُنَا إِلَى الْأَبَدِ..." اقْتَرَبَ مِنْهَا أَكْثَرَ وَقَبَّلَهَا مُرْتَعِشًا، ثُمَّ أَخْرَجَ السُّمَّ مِنْ جَيْبِهِ وَسَكَبَهُ فِي فَمِهِ وَارْتَمَى إِلَى جَانِبِ جُولِييت جُثَّةً هَامِدَةً.

وَصَلَ لُورِنْسْ إِلَى الْمَقْبَرَةِ، فَاعْتَرَضَهُ بِالْتِهَازَارْ فِي الْمَدْخَلِ، فَسَأَلَهُ لُورِنْسْ فِي تَعَجُّبٍ: "مُنْذُ مَتَى وَأَنْتَ هُنَا يَا بُنَيَّ؟"

"مُنْذُ نِصْفِ سَاعَةٍ... لَقَدْ جِئْتُ مَعَ سَيِّدِي" أَجَابَهُ بِالْتِهَازَارْ.

"وَمَنْ يَكُونُ سَيِّدُكَ؟"

"رُومْيُو."

"رُومْيُو؟ يَا إِلَهِي! هَذِهِ مُصِيبَةٌ! حَسَنًا... اِبْقَ أَنْتَ هُنَا وَسَأَدْخُلُ وَحْدِي حَسَنًا؟ أَشْعُرُ أَنَّ مُصِيبَةً قَدْ حَلَّتْ بِنَا!"

هَرَعَ لُورِنْسْ إِلَى الْمَقْبَرَةِ، فَوَجَدَ أَسْلِحَةً مُلَطَّخَةً بِالدِّمَاءِ مَلْقِيَّةً عَلَى الْأَرْضِ وَقَبْرَ جُولِييت مَفْتُوحًا، فَأَلْقَى بِنَظْرَةٍ إِلَى دَاخِلِ الْقَبْرِ لِيَجِدَ جُثَّةَ

رُومِيُو وَبِجَانِبِها جُثَّةَ بَارِيس. وَلَمْ يَكَدْ لُورِنْس يَسْتَوْعِبُ الصَّدْمَةَ حَتَّى اسْتَفَاقَتْ جُولِييت مِنْ نَوْمِها الْعَمِيقِ، فَوَجَدَتِ الْقِسِّيسَ إِلَى جَانِبِها فَسَأَلَتْهُ فِي ذُعْرٍ: "أَيْنَ زَوْجِي؟ أَيْنَ رُومِيُو؟ أَيْنَ هُوَ؟"

وَقَبْلَ أَنْ يُجِيبَها سَمِعَا أَصْوَاتًا مُخْتَلِطَةً تَقْتَرِبُ مِنْهُما فَقَالَ لَها مُسْرِعًا: "شَاءَتِ الْأَقْدَارُ أَنْ تَمْنَعَ مُخَطَّطَنا... زَوْجُكِ قَدْ مَاتَ... ها هُوَ مُلْقًى بِجَانِبِكِ... انْظُرِي!" وَأَشَارَ إِلَى جُثَّةِ رُومِيُو "وَهُنا بِجَانِبِهِ بَارِيس... وَالْآنَ هَيَّا تَعَالِي مَعِي لَقَدِ اقْتَرَبَ الْحُرَّاسُ مِنَّا... هَيَّا مَعِي سَتَلْتَحِقِينَ بِدَيْرِ الرَّاهِبَاتِ..."

"لَنْ أَذْهَبَ مَعَكَ إِلَى أَيِّ مَكَانٍ! اِبْتَعِدْ عَنِّي!" رَدَّتْ جُولِييت فِي حِقْدٍ. فَذَهَبَ لُورِنْس مُسْرِعًا لِأَنَّ الْأَصْوَاتَ اقْتَرَبَتْ مِنْهُما أَكْثَرَ.

نَظَرَتْ جُولِييت إِلَى رُومِيُو وَلَمَحَتِ التِّرْيَاقَ فِي يَدِهِ، فَفَهِمَتْ كُلَّ شَيْءٍ. أَرَادَتْ أَنْ تَشْرَبَ مِنَ السُّمِّ إِلَّا أَنَّها لَمْ تَجِدْ شَيْئًا... لَقَدْ شَرِبَهُ كُلَّهُ. فَأَخَذَتْ خِنْجَرَهُ فِي يَأْسٍ وَغَرَسَتْهُ فِي صَدْرِها وَارْتَمَتْ فَوْقَ زَوْجِها.

وَهُنا، دَخَلَ الْحُرَّاسُ وَخَادِمُ بَارِيس الْمَقْبَرَةَ لِيَكْتَشِفُوا قَبْرَ جُولِييت مَفْتُوحًا وَجُثَّتَها مُلَطَّخَةً بِدِمَائِها بِجَانِبِ جُثَثِ بَارِيس وَرُومِيُو. اِلْتَحَقَ

بِهِمُ الْأَمِيرُ وَوَالِدا جُولِييت وَوَالِدُ رُومْيُو الَّذِي تَرَمَّلَ مُنْذُ أَيَّامٍ بِسَبَبِ حُزْنِ زَوْجَتِهِ عَلَى فِرَاقِ ابْنِها وَنَفْيِهِ مِنَ الْمَدِينَةِ. بَيْنَما قَبَضَ الْحُرَّاسُ عَلَى الْقِسِّيسِ وَعَلَى خَادِمِ رُومْيُو لِلْإِدْلَاءِ بِشَهَادَتِهِما. عَايَنُوا الْجُثَثَ واكْتَشَفُوا أَنَّ جُولِييت ماتَتْ حَدِيثًا.

اِنْهارَ السَّيِّدُ كابوليت وَزَوْجَتُهُ لَدَى رُؤْيَةِ جُثَّةَ ابْنَتِهِما وَدِماؤُها لا تَزالُ تَسِيلُ، في حِينِ صُعِقَ السَّيِّدُ مُنْتَغْيُو لِمَشْهَدِ ابْنِهِ مَيِّتًا. وارْتَفَعَتِ الْأَصْواتُ وَعَلا الصُّراخُ وَالنَّحِيبُ، فَصاحَ الْأَمِيرُ في الْجَمِيعِ: "اِخْرَسُوا! يَجِبُ أَنْ أَعْرِفَ كُلَّ تَفاصِيلِ هَذِهِ الْجَرِيمَةِ الْبَشِعَةِ ثُمَّ سَأَتَّخِذُ جَمِيعَ الْإِجْراءاتِ اللَّازِمَةِ... أَيْنَ هُمُ الْمُتَّهَمُونَ؟"

تَقَدَّمَ الْقِسِّيسُ لورنس مُرْتَعِشًا وَقالَ: "أَنا يا مَوْلايَ الْمُذْنِبُ الرَّئِيسِيُّ في كُلِّ ما حَصَلَ... أَنا السَّبَبُ في هَذِهِ الْمَجْزَرَةِ... سَأَخْتَصِرُ الْحِكايَةَ لِأَنَّها طَوِيلَةٌ جِدًّا! رُومْيُو الَّذِي تَرَوْنَهُ أَمامَكُمُ الْآنَ جُثَّةً هامِدَةً هُوَ زَوْجُ جُولِييت!" صُعِقَ الْجَمِيعُ بِالْخَبَرِ إِلَّا أَنَّ لورنس واصَلَ قائِلًا: "نَعَمْ! رُومْيُو يَكُونُ زَوْجَ جُولِييت! لَقَدْ عَقَدْتُ قِرانَهُما بِنَفْسِي يَوْمَ ماتَ تَيْبالْتُ وَنُفِيَ رُومْيُو مِنْ مَدِينَةِ فيرونا وَأُجْبِرَتْ جُولِييت عَلَى الزَّواجِ مِنْ باريس... قَصَدَتْنِي الْمِسْكِينَةُ جُولِييت في يَأْسٍ عَلَّنِي أَجِدُ لَها حَلًّا يَمْنَعُ زَواجَها الثَّاني... وَهَدَّدَتْنِي بِقَتْلِ نَفْسِها... وَكانَتْ

فِعْلًا سَتُقْدِمُ عَلَى قَتْلِ نَفْسِها بِخَنْجَرٍ، فَأَعْطَيْتُها يا مَوْلايَ عَقاقيرَ مُنَوِّمَةً تَجْعَلُها تَنامُ وَكَأَنَّها مَيِّتَةٌ... وَطَلَبْتُ مِنْها أَنْ تَتَناوَلَها لِيَظُنَّ الْجَميعُ أَنَّها ماتَت، ثُمَّ يَلْتَحِقُ بِها روميو إِلَى الْمَقْبَرَةِ، وَيَنْتَظِرَها إِلى أَنْ تَسْتَيْقِظَ وَيَهْرُبا مَعًا... فَكَتَبْتُ رِسالَةً إِلى روميو أَخْبَرْتُهُ فيها بِالْمُخَطَّطِ، وَأَرْسَلْتُها لَهُ مَعَ صَديقي الرّاهِبِ ذجون، إِلّا أَنَّ هذا الْأَخيرَ فَشِلَ في إيصالِها... فَأَتَيْتُ بِنَفْسي إِلى هُنا... وَلكِنَّني جِئْتُ مُتَأَخِّرًا... وَصَلْتُ إِلى هُنا وَقَدْ كانَ روميو تَخاصَمَ مَعَ باريس وماتا الاثْنانِ... أَظُنُّ أَنَّ روميو قَتَلَ باريس ثُمَّ انْتَحَرَ حُزْنًا عَلى جولييت. ثُمَّ اسْتَيْقَظَتْ جولييت لِتَجِدَ نَفْسَها مُحاطَةً بِجُثَّتَيْهِما. وَعِنْدَما سَمِعْنا أَصْواتَ الْحُرّاسِ، أَخْبَرْتُها بِكُلِّ ما حَصَلَ وَاخْتَبَأْتُ... أَمّا هِيَ، فَرَفَضَتْ أَنْ تَأْتِيَ مَعي... وَوَضَعَتْ حَدًّا لِحَياتِها... هذِهِ هِيَ كُلُّ الْحَقيقَةِ يا مَوْلايَ! وَأُعْلِمُكُمْ أَيْضًا أَنَّ الْمُرَبِّيَةَ عَلى عِلْمٍ بِكُلِّ شَيْءٍ... وَهيَ شاهِدَةٌ عَلى زَواجِ جولييت بِروميو! وَالآنَ... عاقِبوني إِنْ كُنْتُ أَسْتَحِقُّ الْعِقابَ..."

وَسَطَ ذُهولِ الْجَميعِ، طَلَبَ الْأَميرُ إِحْضارَ بِالْتِهازار الَّذي واصَلَ في الاعْتِرافِ قائِلًا: "لَقَدْ أَخْبَرْتُ سَيِّدي روميو بِمَوْتِ زَوْجَتِهِ جولييت... فَأَتى إِلى هُنا وَأَعْطاني رِسالَةً لِأُسَلِّمَها إِلى والِدِهِ... وَهَدَّدَني بِالْقَتْلِ

إِنْ لَمْ أَذْهَبْ وَأَتْرُكَهُ لِوَحْدِهِ..."

وَمِنْ جِهَتِهِ، رَوَى حَارِسُ بَارِيسَ كُلَّ مَا حَصَلَ فِي اللَّيْلِ.

أَخَذَ الْأَمِيرُ الرِّسَالَةَ مِنْ يَدِ بَالْتَهَازَارَ وَفَتَحَهَا. كَانَتِ الرِّسَالَةُ تُؤَكِّدُ كَلَامَ لُورِنْس فَقَالَ الْأَمِيرُ فِي غَضَبٍ: "أَيْنَ هُمْ هَؤُلَاءِ الْأَعْدَاءُ؟ أَيْنَ أَنْتُمْ أَيُّهَا الْأَعْدَاءُ الْمُتَوَحِّشُونَ؟ انْظُرُوا مَاذَا فَعَلْتُمْ بِعِدَائِكُمْ وَكَرَاهِيَّتِكُمْ... سَوْفَ تُعَاقَبُونَ كُلُّكُمْ!"

وَسَطَ كُلِّ هَذَا الْحُزْنِ، احْتَضَنَ السَّيِّدُ كَابُولِيتْ اَلسَّيِّدَ مُنْتَغْيُو وَتَصَالَحَا. وَوَعَدَ السَّيِّدُ مُنْتَغْيُو أَنْ يُشَيِّدَ تِمْثَالًا لِجُولِيتْ مِنَ الذَّهَبِ الْخَالِصِ، وَأَنْ يَنْصِبَهُ فِي قَلْبِ فِيرُونَا. فَوَعَدَ السَّيِّدُ كَابُولِيتْ أَنْ يُشَيِّدَ

تِمْثالًا لِرومْيو أَيْضًا إِحْياءً لِذِكْرى قِصَّةِ حُبِّ روميو وَجولييت.

وَهنا، قالَ الْأَميرُ: "لَقَدِ اسْتَفَقْنا هذا الصَّباحَ عَلى مُصالِحَةٍ عاتِمَةٍ... وَعَلى سِلْمٍ أَسْوَدٍ حَزينٍ... حَتَّى الشَّمْسُ أَبَتْ أَنْ تُشْرِقَ... هَيّا بِنا لِنَذْهَبَ مِنْ هُنا! سَيُكْمِلُ الْحَديثَ في الْأَمْرِ لاحِقًا... هُنالِكَ مَنْ سَيُعاقَبُ... وَهُنالِكَ مَنْ سَيُغْفَرُ لَهُ... أَمّا أَنا، فَلَمْ أَسْمَعْ وَلَمْ أُشاهِدْ مِنْ قَبْلُ حِكايَةً مُؤْلِمَةً وَحَزينَةً كَحِكايَةِ روميو وَجولييت."

# Vocabulary

### p. 138

كابوسٌ (كَوابيسُ) nightmare
أَحْيا [4d] (إحياءٌ) to revive, bring back to life; to celebrate commemorate
حَلَّلَ [2s] (تَحْليلٌ) to analyze

بالْتَهَزارْ Balthasar *(name)*
اِنْقَضَّ عَلَى [7g] to pounce on
جَيِّدٌ good

### p. 139

وارَى [3d] to hide, conceal
جِسْمٌ (أَجْسامٌ) body
تُرابٌ (أَتْرِبَةٌ) soil; dust
طَفا طَفْوٌ [1d3] to float
عَساهُ possibly, might
نَقَلَ [1s3] (نَقْلٌ) to convey, communicate
سامَحَ [3s] to forgive
اِصْفَرَّ [9s] to turn yellow
تَبَخَّرَ [2s] to be perfumed
تَحَطَّمَ [5s] to evaporate, turn to smoke
تَماسُكَ [6s] (تَماسُكٌ) to hold oneself together, remain calm
وَرَقٌ *coll.* paper
حِبْرٌ (حُبورٌ) ink

جَوادٌ (جِيادٌ) horse
حُجْرَةٌ (حُجُراتٌ) chamber, room
صَيْدَلِيٌّ pharmacist
أَتْقَنَ [4s] to master, be skilled at
دَواءٌ (أَدْوِيَةٌ) remedy; medicine
عَقاقيرُ *pl.* drugs, medicine
سامٌّ poisonous, toxic
بَيْعٌ (بُيوعٌ) sale, selling
مَنْعٌ prohibition
باتٌّ definite, definitive
عِقابٌ punishment
قِطْعَةٌ (قِطَعٌ) piece; coin
نَقْدِيٌّ monetary
ذَهَبِيٌّ golden
جُرْعَةٌ dose
قَبْرٌ (قُبورٌ) grave

## p. 140

| | |
|---|---|
| ذُجون John (name) | هَلَعٌ panic |
| [4a1] أَوْصَلَ (إيصالٌ) to deliver | [4d] أَرْسَى to anchor, fix firmly |
| مُتَأَسِّفًا sorrowfully | [2s] خَفَّفَ عَنْ to ease, lighten |
| عَوْنٌ (أَعْوانٌ) agent, official | [1s3] نَثَرَ (نَثْرٌ) to scatter |
| صِحَّةٌ health | [8s1] اِرْتَبَكَ to be confused |
| [1s3] عَبَرَ (عُبورٌ) to cross | بِقُرْبِ near |
| وَباءٌ (أَوْبِئَةٌ) epidemic | ضَريحٌ (أَضْرِحَةٌ) shrine, tomb |
| [8s1] اِنْتَشَرَ to spread | [2s] سَلَّمَ إِلَى to deliver to, hand over to |
| عالِقٌ stuck | |

## p. 141

| | |
|---|---|
| بُعْدٌ (أَبْعادٌ) distance | [3s] عوقِبَ pass. to be punished |
| شَرِسٌ cruel, surly | شَنيعٌ (شُنُعٌ) heinous |
| أَغْلَى elative dearest; most expensive | حِقْدٌ (حُقودٌ) rancor, spite, hatred |
| [1s2] مَلَكَ (مُلْكٌ) to have | [8s1] اِرْتَكَبَ to commit, perpetrate |
| حَقيرٌ (حُقَراءُ) despicable, despised | جَريمَةٌ (جَرائِمُ) crime |
| مَجْنونٌ (مَجانينُ) crazy | حِمايَةٌ protection |

## p. 142

| | |
|---|---|
| [8s1] اِرْتَعَشَ to shudder | [1h2(a)] جاءَ (مَجيءٌ) to come |
| جَيْبٌ (جُيوبٌ) pocket | [1g3] حَلَّ بِ to befall, happen to |
| [1s3] سَكَبَ (سَكْبٌ) to pour | مُلَطَّخٌ stained |
| فَمٌ (أَفْواهٌ) mouth | مُلْقًى thrown, strewn |
| مَدْخَلٌ (مَداخِلُ) entrance | |

## p. 143

| | |
|---|---|
| [10s] اِسْتَوْعَبَ to contain, have the capacity for | قَدَرٌ (أَقْدارٌ) fate, destiny |
| مُخْتَلِطٌ mixed | مُخَطَّطٌ plan, that which is planned |

دَيْرٌ (أَدْيَارٌ) monastery, convent
غَرَسَ فِي [1s2] (غَرْسٌ) to plant in

صَدْرٌ (صُدورٌ) chest

p. 144

تَرَمَّلَ [5s] to become widowed
قَبَضَ عَلَى [1s2] (قَبْضٌ) to arrest, seize
أَدْلَى بِ [4d] (إِدْلَاءٌ) to make (a statement), deliver, present
عايَنَ [3s] to examine, inspect
عَلَا [1d3] (عُلُوٌّ) to become louder/higher

خَرِسَ [1s4] (خَرَسٌ) to become silent
إِجْرَاءٌ step, measure
تَقَدَّمَ [5s] to advance, move forward
مَجْزَرَةٌ (مَجَازِرُ) massacre
أُجْبِرَ [4s] pass. to be forced (in)to

p. 145

مُنَوِّمٌ sleep-inducing, somnifacient
فَشِلَ فِي [1s4] (فَشَلٌ) to fail at
اِنْتَحَرَ [8s1] to commit suicide
مُحَاطَةٌ surrounded by

وَضَعَ حَدًّا لِ [1a1] (وَضْعٌ) to put an end to
أَعْلَمَ [4s] to inform
شاهِدٌ (شَواهِدُ) witness
اِعْتِرافٌ confession, acknowledgment, admission

p. 146

وَمِنْ جِهَتِهِ for one's part; in turn
رَوَى [1d2] (رِوايَةٌ) to tell, recount
أَكَّدَ [2s(a)] to confirm
عِداءٌ animosity, hostility

شَيَّدَ [2s] to build, construct, erect
تِمْثالٌ (تَماثيلُ) statue
ذَهَبٌ gold
خالِصٌ pure, plain, unmixed
نَصَبَ [1s3] (نَصْبٌ) to raise, erect

p. 147

ذِكْرَى memory
مُصالَحَةٌ reconciliation
عاتِمٌ dark, gloomy

شَرَقَ [1s3] to rise
أَكْمَلَ [4s] to complete, finish

مُؤْلِم agonizing, grievous; painful

# Translation

*p. 138*

Romeo woke up from a dream he had at night; he did not seem to understand if it was a beautiful dream or a nightmare. He dreamed that he had died and that Juliet approached him and kissed him and brought him back to life.

And while he was trying to analyze his dream, his servant Balthasar came in, and Romeo pounced on him with questions. "Is there any news from Verona? How is my wife? Is she good? Please, tell me!"

*p. 139*

"What do you want me to tell you, sir? Should I tell you that your wife is buried now? Or do I tell you that your wife's soul is now floating with the angels over the tomb of the Capulets? Yes! Juliet is dead. I witnessed her burial. My heart breaks with pain for you, sir. But what should I do? I must tell you the news. I apologize to you, sir. Please, forgive me."

Romeo nearly went mad at the horror of the news. His face became pale, his eyes turned red, and he felt as if the world was falling around him, his dreams fading in front of him, and his hopes crashing over his head. He tried to hold himself together a little, and he asked his servant to bring him paper and ink to write a letter and a horse to ride. Balthasar obeyed his master, while he stayed in his room alone, weeping over his wife. Suddenly, an idea crossed his mind. And so, he rushed out and went to a poor pharmacist who was skilled at preparing drugs and poisons. The sale of these drugs was strictly prohibited in the city, and the penalty for all those who sold them was death, but Romeo convinced him with gold coins, and he got a toxic dose, and went to Juliet's tomb.

*p. 140*

༶ ༶ ༶

In the meantime, Friar Lawrence had met his friend Friar John and asked him if he had delivered the message to Romeo. But he answered with sorrow, "No, I have not been able to deliver it. Health officers prevented me and another priest from crossing into Mantua because of a serious epidemic that has affected many people. They thought we were in a house where this epidemic was spreading. I am stuck here. Here is your letter." And he gave the letter to Lawrence, who was horrified to hear this bad news. He decided to go to the cemetery so that Juliet would not find herself alone when she woke up, but before that, he began to write a new letter to Romeo to inform him of the updated news.

When night cast its darkness on the city of Verona, Paris went with his servant to the cemetery. He took roses with him hoping to ease his sorrows. He scattered roses on Juliet's grave and continued to weep bitterly. Suddenly, his servant interrupted him. "Sir! sir! Be carerful, there is someone approaching us with a torch!" Paris rose and hid with his servant to observe what was happening. It was Romeo approaching little by little, accompanied by Balthasar.

Romeo stood near Juliet's tomb and gave a letter to Balthasar, saying, "Take this letter and tomorrow morning you must hand it over to my father…

*p. 141*

Now I will go down into Juliet's tomb to embrace her and say goodbye to her… so be careful not to stop me or I'll kill you. Is this understood? And now go and get out of my face!"

The servant left but hid to watch Romeo from a distance while he began to open Juliet's tomb, talking to himself, "You, cruel death! You have robbed me of the most precious thing I have, and now I am offering you my soul, too."

Paris heard him, so he came out from his hiding place in astonishment and shouted, "You bastard, Montague! Do you take your revenge on the dead? Are you crazy? Come with me now! And immediately! You must be punished for your heinous act! You must die!"

Romeo looked at him in hatred and answered, "Please, go away. I do not want to commit another crime. Get away from me immediately!"

Paris refused to move away from Romeo, so they started to fight violently… and it ended with the death of Paris. The servant of the latter rushed to bring the guards to protect his master, not noticing that his master had already died.

*p. 142*

As for Romeo, he went back to opening Juliet's tomb. He looked at her face and cried saying, "My beloved wife, you are so beautiful. Death has taken your breath, but it could not take your beauty. Do not be afraid. I will stay at your side, and I will not leave you. I will stay here forever." He got closer to her and kissed her, trembling, and then he took the poison out of his pocket and poured it into his mouth and fell dead close to Juliet.

Lawrence arrived at the cemetery and he found Balthasar at the entrance. Lawrence asked him in wonder, "How long have you been here, son?"

"For half an hour. I came with my master," Balthasar

answered.

"Who is your master?"

"Romeo."

"Romeo? Oh my God! This is a disaster! Well... stay here and I'll go in alone, alright? I feel that some disaster has befallen us."

Lawrence rushed to the cemetery and found blood-stained weapons lying on the ground and Juliet's tomb open. He looked into the tomb to find Romeo's body...

*p. 143*

and the body of Paris. Lawrence could barely absorb the shock until Juliet woke up from her deep sleep and found the priest next to her. She asked him in panic, "Where is my husband? Where is Romeo? Where is he?"

Before he answered, they heard voices approaching them, and he said to her quickly, "Fate has prevented our plan. Your husband has died. Here he is, lying next to you. Look!" He pointed to the body of Romeo "And here beside him is Paris. Now come with me, the guards are getting closer to us. Come with me. You will join the sisterhood of holy nuns."

"I will not go anywhere with you! Stay away from me!" replied Juliet in hatred, and Lawrence went quickly because the voices had come closer.

Juliet looked at Romeo, and saw the potion in his hand and she understood everything. She wanted to drink from the poison, but she did not find any left. He had drunk it all. She took his dagger in despair and stabbed herself in the chest and fell on top of her husband.

Here, the guards and the servant of Paris entered the cemetery to discover Juliet's tomb open, her body stained with her blood, next to the bodies of Paris and Romeo...

*p. 144*

The prince, Juliet's father, and Romeo's father, whose wife had died few days before out of grief over Romeo's banishmenet, entered along with them, while the guards seized the priest and Romeo's servant so they could testify. They examined the bodies and discovered that Juliet had just recently died.

Lord Capulet and his wife collapsed when they saw the body of their daughter and her blood was still flowing, while Lord Montague was shocked at the sight of his son dead. Voices got louder, along with shouting and crying, so the prince shouted at them, "Be silent! I have to know all the details of this horrible crime. Where are the accused ones?"

Friar Lawrence came closer, trembling, and said, "I am the main culprit in all that has happened. I am the reason for this massacre. I will sum up the story because it is too long! Romeo, whom you now see in front of you as a dead body, is Juliet's husband!" Everyone was shocked by the news, but Lawrence continued, "Yes! Romeo is Juliet's husband! I married them myself the day Tybalt died and Romeo was exiled from the city of Verona and Juliet was forced to marry Paris. Poor Juliet came to me to find a solution to prevent her second marriage and she threatened to kill herself. She was…

*p. 145*

really going to kill herself with a dagger. I gave her, your Highness, sleep-inducing drugs that make her sleep as if dead, and I asked her to take them so everyone would think she was dead, and then Romeo would join her in the tomb and wait for her to wake up and they would run away together. So, I wrote a letter to Romeo telling him the plan and I sent it with my friend Monk John, but he failed to deliver it. I came here myself… but I came too late. I arrived here when Romeo had already fought with Paris and they had both died. I think Romeo killed Paris and then committed suicide out of grief over Juliet. Then Juliet woke up to find herself surrounded by their bodies. When I heard the voices of the guards, I told her everything that had happened and I hid, but she refused to come with me, and then she put an end to her life. This is the whole truth, your Highness! I also inform you that the nanny was aware of everything. She is a witness to Romeo and Juliet's marriage! And now... punish me if I deserve punishment."

While everyone was astonished, the prince summoned Balthasar, who continued the confession, saying, "I told my master Romeo about the death of his wife, Juliet. And so he came here and gave me a letter to give to his father and threatened to kill me...

*p. 146*

if I did not go and leave him alone."

As for Paris's guard, he also recounted everything that had happened that night.

The Prince took the letter from Balthasar's hand and opened it. The letter confirmed Lawrence's words and the prince said in anger, "Where are these enemies? Where are you, savage enemies? Look what you have done with your hostility and your hatred. You will be punished!"

Amidst all this sadness, Lord Capulet embraced Lord Montague and they reconciled. Lord Montague promised to build for Juliet a statue in pure gold and put it up in the heart of Verona. Lord Capulet promised also to build a statue of Romeo...

*p. 147*

to commemorate the love story of Romeo and Juliet.

And then, the Prince said, "We have woken up this morning at a gloomy reconciliation... and at a black and sad peace. Even the sun has refused to shine. Let's get out of here! We will finish talking about this later. There are those who will be punished, and those who will be forgiven. As for me, I have never heard or seen such an agonizing, sad story as the story of Romeo and Juliet."

Visit our website for information on current and upcoming titles, free excerpts, and language learning resources.

# www.lingualism.com

www.ingramcontent.com/pod-product-compliance
Lightning Source LLC
Chambersburg PA
CBHW020123130526
44591CB00032B/405